READING THE RACE

READING THE RACE

Bicycle Racing from Inside the Peloton

JAMIE SMITH

WITH CHRIS HORNER

BOULDER, COLORADO

velopress®

3002 Sterling Circle, Suite 100
Boulder, Colorado 80301-2338 USA
(303) 440-0601 · Fax (303) 444-6788 · E-mail velopress@competitorgroup.com

Distributed in the United States and Canada by Ingram Publisher Services

A Cataloging-in-Publication record for this book is available from the Library of Congress.
ISBN 978-1-937715-10-6

For information on purchasing VeloPress books, please call (800) 811-4210, ext. 2138, or visit www.velopress.com.

This paper meets the requirements of ANSI/NISO Z39.48-1992 (Permanence of Paper).

Cover illustration, cover design, and interior illustrations by Charlie Layton
Interior design and composition by Erin Farrell / Factor E Creative

Text set in Sentinel

13 14 15 / 10 9 8 7 6 5 4 3 2 1

CONTENTS

PREFACE

Bike race announcers see all.

We see all every single weekend from March through September. From our vantage point on the stage, we see all of the full range of racing ability as we announce Category V races, Pro/I/II races, and every race in between.

If we're doing our job correctly, we also say all. We're equal part teacher, cheerleader, traffic controller, and master of ceremonies.

We have the best seat in the house and watch much more racing each year than anyone else, save only the officials.

We each have our own way of explaining what's happening in a bike race to those who are standing on the curb behind the barricades. As a result of all that talking, we become ad hoc experts on bike racing, whether we've ever turned the pedals or not.

I've turned the pedals. As a fair-to-middling bike racer since 1983, I've been on both sides of the barricade. And though I love to stand at the finish line and talk into a microphone, I am much more at home in the middle of a fast-moving peloton. There is an indescribable rush of excitement that can be found only in a bike race. Even if that race consists of just eight masters racers tooling along at 22 mph, sign me up; it is still a bike race. If that bike race consists of 120 racers on an eight-corner criterium in the rain, sign me up! If that bike race consists of one rider on a time trial bike competing against an unseen clock, well, I suppose I could do that, too. If I must.

Bike racing has become much more scientific in recent years. Bicycle design, rider nutrition, and training methods have advanced greatly in the past 15 years. Of course, advances of any sort will give you an edge only until everyone else catches on to them. The first rider who had carbon-fiber wheels had the lightweight advantage for about six days. By the time the next race rolled around, almost everyone had them. Training to power is another technological advancement that has become the preferred training method, but it alone doesn't win races.

I would argue that in the scientific rush forward, much of the nuance of bike racing has been lost. The subtleties of pack riding, bike handling, and butt kicking have been usurped by wattage, functional threshold power, and kilojoules.

Those are important, but you still need to know how to race.

The topic of bike racing tactics really deserves a full set of encyclopedias to catalog and explain every technique, method, rule, trick, and strategy. Unfortunately, no one has time to compile such a collection of data because anyone who would have even a passing interest in doing so is too busy training for his or her next race.

What follows, then, is a fairly detailed explanation of bike racing tactics and techniques based on my many days on the stage as a bike race announcer and many days of suffering at the back of the peloton (due in large part to spending too many days on the stage and not enough days training. Well, at least that's been my excuse since 1983).

Jamie Smith

ACKNOWLEDGMENTS

There are many things I love about bike racing, but one that pertains to writing a book is the ability to call up friends I've known through bike racing for 25 years to talk about a bike race that happened 20 years ago, and their recollection is as clear as crystal and their willingness to help is unbridled. Couldn't have done it without the input of friends/racers/teammates whom I've known for a long time: George Bellairs, John Sammut, Ray Dybowski, Dave Stanley, Brad Sohner, Dale Hughes, Scott Dombrowski, Bryan Adams, Clark Sheehan, Paul Alman, Jeff Noftz, Robin Farina, Mike Tamayo, Steve Mlujeak, and, of course, Chris Horner. And my bike race–announcing mentors who taught me how to really watch a bike race and translate it to the fans: Jeff Roake, Gypsy Patton, Al McDonald, and Beth Wren-Estes. Also, the people at VeloPress who simply know how to make good books: Renee Jardine, Ted Costantino, and Connie Oehring.

Were it not for these people, I would have written a Broadway musical.

1

WHAT'S MY MOTIVATION?

"RIDERS READY," THE CHIEF REFEREE DECLARES. Bang goes the gun, and you're off on the greatest adventure of your life.

Within seconds, you're riding as if launched from a cannon. By the time you reach the first turn, you're completely out of breath. Spectators are a blur on the sidewalk. Two hundred tires on pavement roar like Niagara Falls. The squeal of brake pads on carbon-fiber rims sends chills down your spine. Your mind struggles to make sense of the overload of messages pouring in. You pass—and are passed by—other racers as you fight your way to the first-class section of this bullet train.

You could be spending your weekend enjoying more civilized, relaxing pursuits. Instead, you're in the middle of this cyclone of bikes and bodies. But why? What brought you here? What motivates a person to race a bicycle?

For most racers, the noise, the blur, the battle, the speed are reason enough. Once you've done it, you cannot get enough of it.

And then there's the thrill of competition. It's a race, and you want to win. Of course you want to win. What other reason is there? Why else would anyone spend all that time, energy, and money? Hour upon hour of repetitive training. More hours and many miles of driving to races. And countless trips to the bike shop to buy the newest, lightest, coolest equipment, of course.

Winning is what it's all about. Legends are born by winning. Movies are made about winners. Books are written about winning. Well, not necessarily this book, but lots of other books.

So much emphasis is placed on winning that you might automatically assume that every rider's goal is to be first across the line. Yet there can be only one winner. And in a pack of 100 riders, how many truly have a legitimate shot at winning? Fifty? Twenty? Ten? Seven? Three?

However it shakes out, there will be 99 losers.

It's safe to say that only a small percentage of any peloton—call it 3 percent—has the wherewithal to actually win a bike race. So the other 97 percent of the field must have other good reasons to roll up to the starting line. They've put a lot of energy and resources into what will be a losing effort.

Clearly, winning isn't the only motivation. It's a good thing, too. Not every rider can have a movie made about him or her. There aren't enough theaters in America—or theatres in Canada.

WHY DO YOU RACE?

So I ask again: Why?

Why ride the thousands of miles it takes to gain speed and fitness? Why scrutinize every morsel of food that you eat? Why miss your nephew's confirmation ceremony? Why live in a constant state of soreness? Why spend the national debt of a small country on fancy equipment made in an even smaller country? Why go to all the trouble if not to win?

Believe it or not, some people don't care about winning. Some people willingly go through all that trouble and make all those sacrifices just because they like to ride their bikes fast in a group that is in a constant state of stress. They like the meaningful push toward a finishing goal, even if that goal is just a strip of duct tape strung across the road and they're the 76th rider to cross it. They have no delusions of winning the race; they just like the scene. The pre-race scene, the post-race scene, and the painful scene in between. The one that carries danger and peril. The scene that's played out at 28 miles per hour. That scene. They love to be in it. Even as extras.

Some actors make a living in Hollywood playing bit parts in the background of movies: the out-of-focus guy throwing a Frisbee in the park, the plainly dressed woman carrying shopping bags up the stairs, the anonymous person walking down the sidewalk. Sure, those background actors may have a secret desire deep down inside. And should the hand of fate yank them into the spotlight, they will willingly accept the role. The same can be said for bike racers. If the stars align and events transpire to put them in position to win a race, they will go for it. But winning is not why they race. They race because it's a thrill.

They can't find the same thrill in a club ride; the stress is absent. If you get dropped during a club ride, it's no big deal. You'll catch up to the group when it stops at the next bagel shop. And in a club ride, not everyone sprints for every city-limit sign. But in a bike race, everyone rides with intent. Everyone adds to the electricity. The electricity is what makes it special.

It carries a certain cachet to say you're a bike racer. It buys you some swaggering rights among those who are unwilling to take the risks involved with racing. It makes you just a little more edgy.

At least we like to think so.

And for some, that's the allure of the sport. To them, wearing a skinsuit (as long as it fits properly) is just that much cooler than wearing a regular kit.

Some racers are competitive, but in an internal way. They aren't too keen on mixing it up in the final sprint. They just want to place ahead of a certain point in the field. They may be the ones who are fighting for the last paying spot on the prize list, or who are sprinting for 50th place. That's their race. They feel good if they finish higher than they did the previous week. Or they may pick a rider who is near their own level of ability and try to finish ahead of that person.

Chris Horner   WHY RACE?

I got my first racing license at the age of 15 and have held one almost every year since then. (If I remember correctly, I may have spent a couple of high school years driving around and chasing the next party rather than the next race.) Now, at 41, I hear the same question every time I'm interviewed: "When will you retire?" And I always respond, "When the legs are no good anymore," because I simply can't imagine a time when I won't want to be at a bike race.

Each time that I arrive at the start of a race, I still have the same feelings passing through me as I did before the very first races back in my amateur days. The feelings start to come over me as the car exits the main road and the first signs of the racecourse start to appear. It's always the same adrenaline rush, with nerves rising and excitement growing. Right away, I look around to see which riders and teams are there; what the course looks like (if possible); how big the crowds are; and, of course, how the weather looks. Whether I was pulling up to a Southern California criterium in my VW Scirocco in 1991 or the start of the Tour de France in our RadioShack Nissan Trek team bus in 2012, the experience is the same. And no matter how many times I've been to the start of a bike race, I am always amazed that the feelings and excitement of those moments never change. Retirement? Not anytime soon. ◾

The Social Scene

Some riders treat the race as a social event. They may peel off in the final laps to avoid the mayhem of the sprint, but they gladly suffer through the previous miles because it fits their need for competition and social interaction. For them, victory lies in being there. Victory lies in racing well and not getting dropped.

Some organized sports allow you to dog it. For instance, if you're playing soccer or lacrosse, you don't really have to run full blast up and down the field on every play; you can jog while the others hustle. You won't get dropped from the game. Your teammates might not like it, but you can get away with it.

The closest thing to dogging it in a bike race is when you sit on the back of the pack with your tongue hanging out during the fast parts and carrying on conversations with other tailgunners during the slow parts. If you can't survive the hammer sessions, you're gone.

There's certainly something to be said for the shared experience of having your body thrashed for 90 minutes and surviving.

There's certainly something to be said for the shared experience of having your body thrashed for 90 minutes and surviving. It's a benchmark that helps us judge our dedication. It's also a challenge. We all know of Category II riders who would have much better results if they would downgrade to Cat. III, but they choose to keep their Cat. II license because that's where the challenge is. It may also be where their friends are.

To that end, it's almost like being in high school in that they want to stay with their graduating class. They all came into the sport at about the same time. They raced together and crashed together as Cat. V racers. They laughed and bonked together as Cat. IV riders. They drove to Superweek together as Cat. III racers. And now they're racing as Cat. II racers, whether they're at the same level within that category or not.

Sure, it's harder. Their training regimen is usually just sufficient to make it possible to hang with their chosen group. They suffer plenty at the hands of the fast guys without tasting the success of a victory salute, but they're happy. Their victory is in doing it, not winning it.

That's cool. The more the merrier.

Fitness

Some people race in order to reach fitness goals. Now, the very sound of that notion makes me laugh. I mean, anyone who knows bike racing knows that it's not exactly the healthiest thing you can do to your body. The out-of-balance muscles; the overdeveloped legs and underdeveloped arms. The overstressed trapezius. The hemorrhoids. The constant threat of broken collarbones. The unwanted effects of concentrated pressure on the perineum.

There are far more damaging sports, of course, but I promised my running friends that I wouldn't bash them in this book.

Nevertheless, cycling, in general, is a great fitness activity. Friendly group rides offer camaraderie. But bike racing forces a certain discipline upon its participants that casual riding doesn't. The pressure riders put on themselves to simply not get dropped can push them much harder than a club ride ever would. Working harder than you ever imagined you could helps build character. Personally, I love the feeling I get after a bike race when I sit motionless in my car for several minutes until I can muster the energy to turn the key and push the gas pedal. I feel like I've grown as a person on those occasions when I have to sit down in the shower after a hard ride. I feel alive when I'm that dead.

For some, "fitness" means shedding weight, and the motivation of weight loss has helped many nonracers drop unwanted pounds after they've taken up cycling. And at some point, the competitive fire that has lain dormant in them

Chris Horner   THE SOCIAL SIDE OF RACING

The social side of bike racing is a huge factor in creating camaraderie and friendship that can last for decades. For me, when I started out in the sport, the feeling always began the moment we loaded into the car for the road trip to the race. I traveled with the same two guys throughout my early amateur years, and that experience shaped not only my racing but also my social view of the sport. Of course, since then, my travel companions and teammates have changed many times over, but the early experiences and the lessons learned have had a huge impact on my career.

The two guys that I always traveled with in my early years were Todd Brydon (a masters national road champion), whom I met for the first time while training in the dark at 5 a.m. around San Diego, and Rich Meeker (a multitime masters national champion in almost everything), whom I met at a Swami's team pizza meeting (Swami was the local bike club). They were doing the 30-plus races at the time but also did the Pro/I/II races, which was why they allowed me to ride in the car with them. Meeker had a knowledge of every racer—I think he even knew most, if not all, of the women racers—plus the officials, mechanics, soigneurs, announcers, and sponsors (for our team as well as everyone else's). As we arrived at each of the races, his window would roll down at the first corner, and if we were lucky, he would only speak to 10 or 20 people before we actually parked the car. Todd was more reserved in his racing knowledge, but his stories on the way to the race always kept the car ride interesting and fun.

The days were about stories—both telling old stories and earning new ones—and having a great time while doing something we all loved.

→

> **THE SOCIAL SIDE OF RACING, CONTINUED**
>
> Bike racing began at this moment to give me many of my closest lifelong friends. From travel buddies to training partners to teammates and even my wife, most of the people in my life are ones I met in the sport, and it is a group of friends and acquaintances that has given me a lifetime of stories and adventures. ◾

for a long time is ignited. What starts as a weight loss program becomes a full-on racing regimen.

That's also cool. As I say, the more the merrier.

To Help Someone Else Win

Now we're getting somewhere.

If only 3 percent of the field has a chance of winning, then the other 97 percent is there to play a role in the outcome in whatever way it is able. There are several ways to do so. Some are obvious. Some are barely noticeable.

The motivation to drive toward a common goal in competition is what makes team sports great. Riders are willing to spend time and energy training, as well as burning every ounce of energy they have during a race, even when they know they don't have a chance of winning. They're willing to throw everything they have out onto the road in order to improve their teammate's chances. And they do this with little or no expectation of tangible reward.

That's some pretty amazing stuff right there.

THE PRO GAME VERSUS OUR GAME

A rider who aspires to reach the pinnacle of the sport that he or she has been watching on television or online may have to relearn some things to compete in local races. Tactically, professional bike racing in Europe is almost unrecognizable when compared to racing at the amateur level in America.

Like you, I watch the spring classics. I watch the grand tours. I'm addicted. Like you, I stream them online at my office when I should be working. I won't tell if you won't.

As I watch those races, I see similarities. I also see, in many ways, a completely different sport.

First of all, helicopters. We don't have them at our industrial-park criteriums. If we did, I'm sure you'd learn to pin your number on securely.

Helicopters have nothing to do with tactics. Culture, however, does.

Euro Pro

In America, when a baby is born, the obstetrician slaps the baby's bare bottom to shock the baby and start the breathing process. In Europe, the obstetrician places the baby's bare bottom on a cold bicycle seat to shock the baby and start the breathing and pedaling process.

In Europe, absorption of bike racing culture begins much earlier than it does in the United States. Cycling clubs for kids are everywhere. Organized racing in some European countries starts at age 6, and the national sanctioning bodies for cycling create a clear path to follow from the amateur ranks to the pros. If you have cycling talent, there are plenty of support systems to help you go as far as you can.

Here in the U.S., however, we see very few racers under the age of 15. In fact, according to recent USA Cycling (USAC) statistics, there are only 4,927 registered riders under the age of 18 in the entire country. Compare that to the 6,000 U.S. Youth Soccer clubs in the country and the five million kids playing baseball in the U.S., according to Little League Baseball and Softball statistics.

The Euro cycling scene begins with the way cycling is not only a part of everyday life but also a major part of professional sports. It is also reflected in the racing that is done over there. Races are longer than races in the States. The amount of television and media coverage is greater. The importance of winning is greater. For many riders, a bike racing career is a ticket away from factory work. American riders will take it as far as they're able, but they're rarely destined to work on a farm if they fail.

That's a fundamental cultural difference between the European pro and an American pro racing in Europe.

As such, the style of racing in the European pro peloton is vastly different from what we see in American amateur racing. In Europe, if a team sponsor wants air time in a telecast, the riders will spend much of their energy to get one of their own into the break du jour. Put a rider on the front and you'll get TV screen time galore and plenty of mentions from the announcers.

European cycling is big business. However, it is also theater. Sometimes what we see in the Tour de France is not what it appears to be. I repeat: sometimes.

For instance, when we tune in to watch stage 12, we see a five-man break-away rolling along the French countryside holding a 10-minute lead over an uninterested peloton. We presume that the riders in the break attacked violently, perhaps on a hill, got a gap, and slowly extended their lead through hard work and a synergistic cooperative effort. That might be true. For the first several kilometers of the stage, I promise you that there was a flurry of attacks. The pace was torrid. Viewed from the helicopter's gyroscopic lens, the pack was shaped like a snake as attack after attack went up the road. As soon as one was reeled in, another vicious attack was launched. And another. And another. And then the yellow jersey stopped to pee.

When the yellow jersey stops for a "nature break," the racing light is extinguished briefly out of deference to the race leader. The field slows down to wait, and whoever happens to be off the front during this stoppage has just been granted break-du-jour status.

Sometimes it's not the maillot jaune that creates the nature break. Sometimes it's the green jersey. Or Mr. Polka Dot. Or one of the other favorites.

The break du jour, meanwhile, is away, gone, up the road, and it will remain there until the team directors start to get nervous.

This type of breakaway never happens at the amateur level of American racing. For one thing, no one is allowed to stop and pee during our races. If the pre-race favorite were to pull off the road to pee, the ensuing attacks would be so violent, bike frames would snap in half. Woe betide the rider who hesitates for a minute in an American bike race, thinking that the field will cut him a break.

In the major leagues, different rules apply.

American Pro

The American professional cyclist is a different animal, a species distinct from both the Euro pro and the American amateur.

The competition to become and remain a professional cyclist in the U.S. is no less intense than it is in Europe. There are hundreds of up-and-coming hotshots who are working hard, hoping to land a pro contract and begin living the dream. But generally, they aren't on a quest for a better life. In fact, knowing what we know about the hardscrabble life of a pro cyclist, the opposite may be true. They are willing to sleep on floors and squeeze eight teammates into a minivan for a 12-hour drive to a shared hotel room in the bad part of town to race. If they get a pro contract, the "dream" that they will enjoy still involves living out of a suitcase for six months, trying to scrape together a decent week of training, juggling airport connections, and fighting the boredom of hotel rooms. But on the plus side, they will know where their next meal is coming from, they will have more than two pair of shorts, and they will have teammates whom they can count on. They won't have to drive to the races, but they will spend more time at baggage claim worrying about whether or not their bike made the trip intact.

It's a hard life.

What we wouldn't give to be living it.

American pro cyclists race a different type of race than we amateurs do. At any point in the race, they can turn to a teammate and tell him to go to the front and reel in the breakaway. And do you know what happens? The teammate goes straight to the front and starts the chase. He has to; he is paid to answer the call. The team members know that there are hundreds of hotshots waiting in the wings who would be willing to do it if they can't. They are paid to train on Thursday mornings so that when their leader turns to them on Sunday, they are ready, willing, and able to crank it up. They can't turn to their team leader and say, "Sorry, man. I got nothin'."

Ya got nothin'? Hmm.

Hello, hotshots? Are you free next weekend?

Amateur racing is much different. It is fast, exciting, dangerous, and hard, but if I turn to one of my teammates and tell him we need to reel in the breakaway, I'm liable to hear any number of responses, none of which shows any promise of accelerating the pace of the peloton.

"No, man, I'm tapering. The state time trial is next weekend."

"Can't. I'm cooked. I played soccer with my daughter all day yesterday."

"You're on your own, dude. I feel like crud."

And if I do get a positive response, will my teammate know what to do once we catch the breakaway? Pro cyclists know exactly what to do because they study it. They're paid to know every tactic available to them and who on their team is best suited for what purpose.

They also know who the strong local riders are when they're racing in Albuquerque, in addition to the other pro riders whom they see every other weekend. And they know which local teams to watch out for when they get to Kenosha. That's also part of being a pro.

Chris Horner   BREAKING INTO THE GLAMOROUS PRO LIFE

For most European riders, if they don't make it to the pro ranks, their life after cycling can be pretty rough. You might be interested to know that for most Americans, life as an aspiring professional—and even for many pros who have made it—can be far from glamorous as well.

My first big road trip was in 1992. We were leaving from Redlands, California, right after the last stage of the Redlands Classic finished and traveling all the way over to Quebec, Canada, to do Tour de Beauce; Tour of Adirondacks in upstate New York; the Olympic trials in Altoona, Pennsylvania; Superweek in Milwaukee; and whatever other local races we could find along the way to fill in the gaps. Our group had five riders and a female soigneur, traveling together for months.

We traveled in a Chevy Astro minivan, donated to us by a local amateur riding club to use for the next three months, and Trent Klasna's Chevy S-10 pickup (standard cab, meaning no backseats). The S-10 was packed to the limit, and the Astro van was packed as well, leaving just enough space for the backseats to recline so that the nondrivers could catch a little sleep between shifts.

If I remember correctly, we only did two or three nights of sleeping in the cars, choosing instead to drive most nights to get to our next host housing or race destination that much sooner. Along the way, the favorite choice for breakfast after a night of sleeping in the cars was the Denny's Grand Slam at $1.99, so with a $1 tip we could make it in and out pretty cheap. We usually kept a few groceries in the cars—soda, sandwiches, and chips—to keep the cost down, but dinner was a daily necessity that cut severely into our meager budgets. Even though gas money

→

BREAKING INTO THE GLAMOROUS PRO LIFE, CONTINUED

and housing (including even a few hotels during the races) were covered, the food costs quickly ate into the few hundred dollars that I had saved at the start of the trip. Luckily for us, we were racing pretty well, and back in those days the races paid the prize money right after the race ended— and usually in cash—helping us to make it through.

If not for the generous host families along the way, there was no way we could possibly have survived the trip. I think I started with $400 or $500 and was down to just over $100 before we even got to the first race. From then on, every race was about survival and literally making it through to the next day. It's a tough life getting started as an American in cycling, but thanks to all of the race organizers, host families, volunteers, and generous people along the way, I was able to survive the transition from an amateur to the biggest stage in cycling: the Tour de France. ▪

American Amateur

Though different from European racing and American professional racing, American amateur racing is still awesome. It's one of the coolest, most challenging recreational pursuits in the country. It is equal parts grueling and beautiful. Not many sports can match bike racing for the wide range of physical pains and raw emotions that it brings to its participants.

As a body of racers, we come from every known profession and vocation. As such, we are all over the map when it comes to motivations, abilities, and objectives.

In a typical cycling club that has a racing component, you will find a wide array of enthusiastic racers spanning all levels of ability and dedication. There are racers who take things very seriously and train almost as much as professional riders train. They participate in every race on the calendar, even if it requires driving 10 hours to get there. It is in this group that we find the aforementioned hotshots who endeavor to climb the ladder as far as possible. You can spot them a mile away: They are enthusiastic. They are talented. They are thin. You will also have riders who intend to ride as much as they can but whose training regimen is interrupted by a cranky boss who has the unmitigated gall to demand that they work a 40-hour week. They might also have families with stringent and unrealistic requirements that they actively participate in the upbringing of their own children. They may own a house that is in constant need of paint. If the house is not in need of paint, the racer will take it upon himself to add on a new room that will eventually require several coats of paint. All of these things conspire to keep the racer from training as hard as necessary. Still, these riders race, and they will be on your team.

You will have teammates who are as strong as an ox but lack a brain.

You will have riders who are as strong as an ox and have all the natural ability in the world but who lack a brain. These are riders who, no matter how many times you tell them not to chase you when you're off the front, will chase you every time you're off the front. They are, as a famous cycling coach once described them, "strong like bull, smart like tractor."

You will also find enigmatic racers in your club who show up once in a blue moon. You won't remember their names because you don't see them often enough. They will appear out of nowhere, and they will expect to be considered a part of the team despite wearing the club's kit from the 1980s.

And then come the dedicated amateurs who train and ride a lot, but not nearly as much as a pro. They have no aspirations of riding on a pro team. Nevertheless, they watch everything they eat. They rest appropriately. They actually ride slow on their easy days and hard on their hard days. They set achievable yet challenging goals. They are dedicated and always wanting more.

Somehow, you're all supposed to come together and ride like a team, using team tactics to beat other teams facing the same challenges.

Another difficult challenge in amateur cycling is that newcomers—women and masters category racers especially—are faced with a steep learning curve. Newbies come into this complex sport and must jump into the deep end of a pool brimming with seasoned veterans who can ride circles around them. The newbies are not worried about team tactics; they're worried about survival. They can hardly get through a 90-degree turn alive, let alone provide a lead-out to your designated sprinter.

Races in the masters category (according to the USAC rule book, anyone older than 35) are often as fast as the top-category races due to the riders' experience and training. There is a mistaken belief that masters racers will take it easy because they all have careers and families to consider. That kind of thinking will get you into trouble. Masters racers are nice on the outside, but their ancestors sailed on Blackbeard's boat.

New masters racers, when faced with the choice of racing with their Cat. IV brothers or with their age group, often make the mistake of believing that the masters race will be easier because they think the old farts will ride slower and will therefore be easier to hang with. That is simply not the case. The masters field is notoriously fast and is full of thieves and pirates who will rob you blind.

I mean that in the best way possible.

Women's racing is much more complex. Women are far more welcoming and embracing of new riders, but they will simply ride away from those who have yet to develop the speed necessary to hang in. The great disparity between abilities in the women's field is amplified by the relatively low number of participants.

Chris Horner SPARE A THOUGHT FOR THE MASTERS

I truly believe that American amateur masters should be classified not just by age but also by the number of kids they have, the number of hours they work, and whether or not they are married. ◧

In some parts of the country where racing is especially popular, new riders may find a more welcoming entry into the racing world. With a greater number of participants, promoters may have the luxury of providing an entry-level race such as a masters Cat. IV race or a women's Cat. IV race, which separates the lambs from the wolves. In parts of California, promoters often embed Cat. II riders into the Cat. V fields to act as rolling mentors to ensure safety and to pass along pointers to the uninitiated. But in most parts of the country, the field sizes are small, forcing promoters to combine fields. That creates a challenge that pro riders certainly never see. For example, pro riders will never have to turn to a new teammate during a race and give instructions on when to shift gears.

MISTAKES AMATEUR TEAMS MAKE

It's a mistake to assume that everyone is on the same page in regard to tactics and strategies, as if bike racing knowledge comes naturally when we buy our first racing bike. It doesn't. And it doesn't come from watching European classics while riding the trainer. Television cameras can't possibly convey the nuances and subtlety involved with team tactics. Race savvy also doesn't come after two or three races; yet many teams will bring in a new rider and expect him or her to learn tactics under fire.

Experienced riders sometimes know tactics so well that they think they're apparent to everyone. True—once you learn them, they do seem obvious. Also, experienced riders are often too busy training to take the time to mentor younger riders.

A team with experienced riders who can share tactical knowledge would be wise to hold regular chalkboard sessions using Xs and Os to diagram the tactics, just as we see coaches doing in other sports. Actually, since cycling is a multiteam sport, you'd need more than Xs and Os. You'd need Ys, Zs, Ns, and pretty much the whole alphabet. And one letter would be dressed in a kit from the 1980s.

There are some elements that can be taught effectively by walking through them in slow motion without the bikes. Football and basketball teams learn their plays this way. The same technique can be used by cyclists to great effect.

But this rarely happens. More often, every training ride turns into a hammerfest/ego competition followed by a sprint to a city-limit sign with little or no instruction on how to win that sprint and no review of how you lost it. You just keep pedaling to the next one.

Individually, many riders fall into the mileage trap and feel that they must ride, ride, and ride some more in order to either maintain or improve their fitness. Few are willing to get off the bike and talk about racing.

I'm generalizing, of course. But in speaking with riders from around the country, I've come to see this is as a common thread. It's human nature to think that more is better, so riders will continue to think that more miles are the best road to success.

Another mistake that amateur teams make is to devise a race plan that is too rigid: "If anything goes up the road, we have to make sure we put Dave in it." Well, that's not even remotely realistic. Especially if Dave burns all of his matches during the first 20 failed attacks. Or, perhaps a more likely scenario, if Dave spent the entire week on his feet at a trade-show booth demonstrating CNC machinery to prospective clients, he'll be fried after the first attack. Either way, Dave is cooked, and we should have a backup plan. In fact, we should have a couple and know how to react to what the other teams are trying to do.

A bike race is a fluid, ever-changing, unpredictable monster that is full of surprises. All of those other teams are plotting to upset your plan.

Some teams will employ the same game plan at every race they attend, and they'll place the same riders into the same role each time. By mid-June, every other team will know what to look for. A little advance planning at that point to create a new strategy can keep the team in the hunt—if the members are smart enough to recognize it.

HOW TACTICS HAVE CHANGED

The race tactics that we see today are quite different than they were 20 or 30 years ago. They're kinder and gentler. That's not to say that bike racing is kind and gentle. It's definitely not, but today's tactics are much more refined than they were in the 1980s.

In my first year of racing, I was in a criterium in which our team missed the breakaway. I went to the front of the field and was trying to get the chase effort started when a rider from a team that hadn't missed the breakaway came alongside me, got his shoulder ahead of my shoulder, and slowly pushed me into the curb, bringing my chase effort to a grinding halt. A teammate of mine took up the chase again, only to be physically hooked into the curb by the same rider.

It's a relief to say that things were done a bit differently then.

Eddie Borysewicz was the American national team coach throughout most of the 1980s. In his 1984 book *Bicycle Road Racing—Complete Program for Training and Competition* (Velo-News 1984), the following passage appears:

> *You must be tough. You must repulse elbows with elbows of your own, but don't fight when you don't need to. Be fair, but don't be chicken. Sometimes you might need to lock your brakes in front*

of the blocker, not to make him crash but to let him know you are a dangerous guy to fool with.

If you bothered me when I was racing, I would hit you with my rear wheel—bang it right into your front wheel and knock you down if you weren't a good bike handler. I would say, "You want to play? What kind of game do you want? I'm ready for anything. C'mon!"

Eddie B. was an authority on racing in the 1980s. Today we teach things differently.

In my early years of racing, I can't remember how many times I felt someone grab my jersey when I was trying to move forward in the pack. Another common tactic from the Dark Ages was to simply push people out of the way. If someone wanted to move forward, they might put their hand on your hip and simply push you to the side, just enough to sneak past you.

Legal? Not at all. But common.

Another "tactic" that I remember seeing on more than a few occasions was for someone to reach over while you were climbing a hill and throw your rear shift lever all the way forward. This would cause your chain to jump onto the smallest cog. Obviously, this was back in the Neolithic era when shift levers were located on the downtube of the bicycle and indexed shifting had not yet been invented. Back then we did stuff like that to win races. Today we wouldn't think of such a thing. Anyway, we wouldn't have the opportunity; it's not as easy to mess with someone else's shifters on the fly.

Older racers also know how to sneak into the pit area and get a free lap without having the requisite mechanical problem to qualify for a free lap. I won't tell you how it's done. I don't wish to corrupt your mind with bad ideas. (See me after class.) I will also say that I have never done it. Not in the past 10 years, anyway.

I also remember in my early years of racing that some riders were notorious for taking their own free laps on the back side of the course. This was easy to do during nighttime criteriums. You could just hide in the shadows on the outside of turn 3 and jump in when the field passed by. Not that I ever tried. I had usually been dropped out of contention long before the idea occurred to me.

Today, if a rider tried some of these tactics, he or she would be met with great opposition. We are more self-policing in the contemporary peloton. We

Chris Horner · HOW TACTICS HAVE CHANGED

Back in the early years, a lot of pushing and shoving certainly existed within the peloton. My introduction to this side of the sport was given to me by Radisa Cubric, a Yugoslavian pro who raced in the States for about five years. It was 1993, and I was riding for an East Coast professional-amateur team. They had flown me to Florida for a four- or five-week training camp in Mount Dora. It was a tiny town with nothing but flat roads and lakes (or possibly swamps, depending on what your definition of one versus the other might be).

The first race we did together was at an overgrown, undeveloped business/residential neighborhood that had nothing finished except for the streets and the curbs. I found this to be quite common in Florida at the time, as we saw it several more times at other races before my trip was up. When the race began, a break immediately formed of about 15 riders, give or take. It was me, a couple of teammates, and a bunch of guys that I, as a West Coaster, had never seen or raced against before. When the bell rang for the first prime, I was on Radisa's wheel as we came out of the last corner. I had never met him before that day. As we

→

HOW TACTICS HAVE CHANGED, CONTINUED

were coming up to the line, he hooked me across four lanes, all the way from the left side of the road to the right, keeping me from winning the prime and almost crashing me. This was directly in front of the officials, who didn't seem to object one bit!

As the break of riders started the rotating paceline once again, I purposely positioned myself on Radisa's wheel so that after he took his pull, I could swing over the top of him and take him straight to the curb. That immediately got his attention, and in response, he reached over and grabbed my ponytail. We proceeded to bump each other down the entire straightaway, almost crashing each other and the rest of the break. In those days, that didn't even get us a stern talking-to from the officials, let alone get us disqualified.

After the race, as Radisa came to our team van, I was sitting in the front passenger seat with my legs stretched out onto the open door. He immediately threatened to rip my head off. I was still a little guy back then, and Radisa was definitely bigger than me—and from the Eastern bloc to boot. Luckily for me, my Irish teammate Paul McCormack jumped between us and probably saved my life. Afterward Paul explained that I should never mess with Radisa because he might actually kill me, and also because hooking was "just bike racing."

The funny thing about the whole story, though, was that not only did I learn a lesson from Radisa Cubric on standard bike racing in those days, but he and I would go on to become good cycling friends. We even got the chance to catch up during the London Olympics in 2012, where he was directing for the Serbian national team and I was riding for the U.S. ■

don't rely on the officials to see all of the infractions. We also don't tolerate the physicality of the old-school tactics.

Those days are gone.

Sigh.

TACTICS OF OTHER SPORTS: A COMPARISON

I like watching the last few minutes of an exciting football game when the trailing team is using the hurry-up offense. With no time-outs remaining, the quarterback must try to communicate with the coach over the din of the crowd. The clock is ticking. The crowd is making it difficult for the players to hear the signal. There's no time to huddle up and get the message to everyone. They must rely on their knowledge of the playbook and their assignments. The frantic nature of this moment is as close as football gets to a bike race.

When the heat is on in a bike race, there's no opportunity to get together with your teammates to discuss your next course of action. You must know the plays thoroughly and be able to convey complex thoughts in three words or less.

When you report to football training camp, your coach will bestow upon you a document more treasured than the Magna Carta. It's called the playbook. It contains all of the plays that your team must know. Guard it with your life.

Football also has well-established positions that are determined early on in a player's life. Regardless of what position you may want to play, you will be placed in the position best suited to your body type by a well-intentioned coach. If you have a good throwing arm, you may find yourself thrust into the role of quarterback at an early age. Big guys will be put on the line of scrimmage. Fast guys will be made into running backs, receivers, or defensive backs. From that day forward, you will become locked in at that position. You may wonder what it's like to play another position, but you will probably never find out.

The same thing happens in baseball. Once you show any kind of aptitude for playing third base, you will forever be typecast as a third baseman. You may have dreams of being a right fielder like your childhood hero (insert name of a famous right fielder here), but your die is cast. In the world of "Who's on First?," your name is "I Don't Know": third base.

It's different in bike racing. You must know all of the tactics on both sides of the ball. They're happening simultaneously. While you may fancy yourself a sprinter, a climber, a rouleur, or a time trial specialist, you will need to know how to play all of the other positions and how to enact all of the tactics that a bike racer must know. Very few amateur teams have the luxury of protecting one rider throughout a race in order to save him or her for that one solitary burst of talent. Unless your name is Mark Cavendish, you can't tell your teammates, "I'm not chasing down that breakaway. I'm a sprinter." If they need your help to chase the breakaway, you must roll up your sleeves and pitch in. Otherwise, you may not get a chance to use your sprint. And if they do accept your diva attitude, you had better deliver the goods when the time comes.

You must, as a cyclist, work on and develop all of the necessary skills. You may be a natural sprinter, but if that's all you can do, your bag of tricks empties quickly.

The deeper your bag of tricks, the more bike races your team will win.

2

BASIC TRAINING

THERE ARE BASIC SKILLS AND TECHNIQUES that all riders must know before they dive into the ocean of complex strategies and tactics. When I talk about those tactics later, I'm going to make a lot of assumptions about your ability to handle the fundamentals. Many of these ideas should be hammered into you when you start riding with a group, and some of them come with time. Taken together, they make you a complete bike racer, so learn them, know them, and live them.

Notice that I didn't say, "Love them." Some you will, and some you won't.

If you're going to be a bike racer, you need to be prepared to handle any situation that comes up. You can't fake it.

I learned this very early in my racing career from a guy who played a role as a extra in the greatest movie ever made, *Breaking Away*. In my mind, his one small acting role (as an out-of-focus guy in the background) gave him instant credibility, so I took his word as gospel. Thirty years later, I haven't found reason to doubt it.

One day he called to ask if I wanted to go for a ride. It was raining hard, and I told him I didn't want to ride in the rain.

"So," he said, "what happens if you drive six hours to get to a bike race and it's raining? Are you going to turn around and drive six hours home?"

Good point, Professor.

I don't like corners. I don't like gravel. I don't like hills. I don't like wind. I don't like descending. I don't like country music.

I just have to learn to deal with it and race my bike.

By the way, I've been in races in which I couldn't stand the music that the announcer was playing over the P.A. system, but I soldiered on. And I'm sure I never played one bad song throughout my own career as an announcer. OK, maybe once.

BIKE HANDLING

A most basic element of bike racing is to have complete control of the bike at all times on every surface at any speed. We know that all bikes have their own handling characteristics that are a function of their material, geometry, and weight distribution. We also know that a minor adjustment in the distribution of weight can have a drastic effect on a bike's handling.

Your bike's personality may change with speed. You must master it no matter what. Your bike needs to feel as comfortable to you at 45 mph as it does at 12 mph. You must have complete confidence in your bike's mechanical condition as well. Everything must work.

You also cannot have any blind spots. A blind spot is a weakness that will be exploited by savvy competitors. For instance, many riders have difficulty negotiating corners at high speeds. Perhaps they have a mental block stemming from a crash long ago, or perhaps their bike just doesn't handle corners well. (That can happen. I've owned bikes that I had to fight through every turn, and I've owned bikes that could go through a corner like they've preridden the course without me. I quickly learned which bikes to ride in which type of race.)

Any situation that you avoid because you lack the skills to tackle it is a blind spot. Many blind spots arise from a lack of practice. If you can't corner well at speed, it may be that you don't practice high-speed cornering enough.

You should practice bike-handling skills often when you're a new racer and periodically when you're seasoned. There are no prescribed workouts for this; you are free to create your own. Basically, you want the bike to become an extension of your body.

For the purposes of this discussion, I'll assume that you're already riding a bike that has been properly and professionally fitted to you by a qualified shop that works with lots of racers. If you haven't been through that process with your bike, you should start there before doing anything else.

CORNERING

If you race in America, you're going to see a lot of courses with 90-degree turns (Figure 2.1). Criteriums dominate the U.S. racing scene, and corners dominate the crit. As such, you will need to master left- and right-hand turns equally.

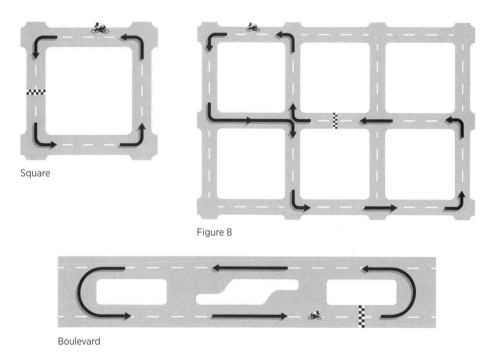

Square

Figure 8

Boulevard

FIGURE 2.1 Criterium racecourses you will encounter

And 180-degree turns in both directions.

And off-camber turns.

And ess curves.

And 137-degree turns with manhole covers in the middle.

All of the above in the rain.

All of the above in the rain at night.

Learn to make all these turns perfectly on your own. You will eventually have to do them while knocking elbows with the rider next to you.

Did that just freak you out a little?

Well, I can't soften it for you. If you are in this sport for more than a day, you will need to become adept at negotiating corners safely and efficiently while in the middle of the cyclone of riders. There's no avoiding it. If you can't corner well, you will only make life hard on yourself. If you're not good at cornering, you will slow down a little bit every time you enter a turn and lose precious momentum. A few riders will probably pass you. As you exit the turn, you will need to accelerate hard to make up the lost speed. In a game that is won by conserving energy until needed, this approach is a losing proposition.

If you're accelerating more than the riders around you, you're working harder in each corner than they are. Multiply that by the number of corners on a course, and it adds up to a lot of wasted energy.

So here is the single most important thing I can tell you about your favorite sport: Conservation of energy is the law of bike racing.

Guard your energy and you will succeed. Waste your energy and you will fail.

Not everything in life is that simple, but bike racing often is.

Learning Cornering Skills

When it comes to learning cornering skills, I'm a fan of visuals. It helps my understanding if I can actually see what's happening to the bike when I go through a corner. I know the bike will naturally tilt as it goes through a turn,

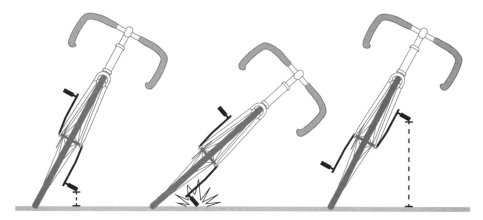

FIGURE 2.2   Cornering lean angles

but how far can I lean it over? A bike can lean more when I'm coasting than it can when I'm pedaling.

Try this: Before you practice riding around corners, get off the bike and stand next to it. Place the pedal nearest you at the bottom of the stroke. Lean the bike toward you. Notice how far it will lean before the pedal scrapes the pavement (Figure 2.2). Get comfortable with this angle. There will come a time when you need to pedal through every corner at high speed, and this angle is the limit. It's not the same for every bike; it changes with frame geometry, pedal type, and crank length.

If you lean over too far while pedaling, you will plant the pedal into the pavement, and the bike will buck like a bronco. You may get lucky and simply scrape your pedal on the pavement, which makes a distinctive sound that'll be followed by some sort of vocal reaction by those around you. Or you may get tossed to the ground.

Still standing by the bike, next rotate the pedal nearest you to the top of the stroke and lean the bike toward you again. This time, without the pedal in the way, it'll lean much farther. This angle also has its limits: When you're coasting, you're limited by the grip of your tires.

Now that you've seen these angles with your own two eyes, get on your bike and explore those limits.

First, you'll want to find a place where you can ride through 90-degree corners without any risk of running into anything or of anything running into you. An empty parking lot or industrial complex will suffice, but I like to use a cemetery for this type of practice. Traffic is light. The occupants don't complain much. The roads are usually in good shape. You will often find a lack of curbing, so if you do happen to run off the road, you'll only run onto the grass. Just try to avoid the headstones. And the World War II cannon located near the flagpole. And the flagpole.

Let's take a simple 90-degree right-hand turn in which the width of the road remains constant (Figure 2.3). You need to approach it from the left curb and make one large, smooth arc through the turn, rounding off the corner as

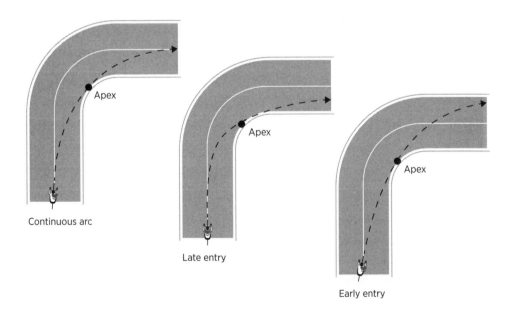

FIGURE 2.3 Cornering lines. The rider here is respecting the center line. If this were a closed-course race, he could use the full width of the road, but the principle would remain the same.

much as possible. This allows the highest possible speed to be maintained. Approaching the apex of the turn too early, too late, or too fast will affect your ability to negotiate the turn. If you make several little turns on your way through the corner, you will scrub off a little bit of speed each time.

The apex, or center of the turn (motorcyclists also call this the clipping point), is the point at which your bike will be leaning the most. At high speeds, you will gain nothing and risk much by pedaling at this point in the turn. Keep your innermost pedal up and wait until you have straightened up before resuming your pedal stroke. You can also gauge your ability to pedal through the corner by watching riders ahead of you. If they're not pedaling, you'd be wise to follow suit.

The act that really initiates the turn is a process called countersteering. At speeds above 12 to 14 mph, your front wheel acts as a gyroscope, so to turn right, you need to gently push forward on your right handlebar, which will cause your bike to begin to lean to the right (a phenomenon known as "precession"). Hold steady forward pressure on the right bar through the corner, and you'll carve a nice arc right through it.

It may seem counterintuitive to actually turn the bars to the left to make the bike turn to the right. You may have been taught simply to lean into a turn. To get the bike to lean, however, takes this initial push on the handlebar. It may feel as if you're pushing the bike out from under you. You are, briefly. Thanks to the gyro effect of the front wheel, it will only be enough to start the lean that will allow the bike to turn.

At speeds above about 14 mph, you can't steer solely by steering, nor can you steer solely by leaning. You have to do both, so it is important to get comfortable with both.

Knowing this process instinctively will give you much more control of the bike. You will be better able to avoid crashes and other hazards. You will also be able to control the lean angle with more precision, and that control will allow you to change your course midturn.

At low speeds, the lean angle is less severe, and you can continue to pedal through the corner. As you increase your speed, your bike will lean farther. At some point, you will need to stop pedaling or risk scraping the inside pedal, the one nearest the inside of the turn.

As you coast through the corner, put weight on the outside pedal to make you more stable. Keeping your torso low will also help keep the bike stable.

Whenever you practice this technique, try to feel what your bike is doing, experiment with your position, get comfortable with the lean, and concentrate on making one sweeping arc through the turn rather than several small arcs. Round off the corner to allow yourself to carry as much speed as possible through the turn. Keeping a constant pressure on the inside handlebar will help immeasurably.

By focusing too intently on an object, you can actually forget about everything else, including how not to hit it.

And here's the most important skill to learn when cornering: Look through the turn. Don't look at the road surface.

Many riders will focus on the pavement just a few feet ahead of them. That's a mistake. It's too late to do anything about that bit of pavement. Instead, you must look through the turn to what's ahead. You can scan the pavement for gravel, sand, cracks, and junk as you approach the turn and make small adjustments to miss any of those things. But don't focus on it too long—use your peripheral vision to keep track of it. If you stare at it, you will ride right into it. Motorcyclists and military fighter pilots call this "target fixation." By focusing too intently on an object, you can actually forget about everything else, including how not to hit it. Motorcyclists in particular live by the phrase "You go where you look." So instead of looking at the ground in front of you, you need to look where you want to go.

Try it. It really works.

After you get comfortable cornering quickly by yourself, find a riding partner to do it with. This will teach you to allow room for another rider.

You can't just do a few corners and say, "I get the idea." Repetition is what will help you become more polished. As you become better at carving an arc through a turn, you can start to experiment with the radius of your arc. You can try to tighten the radius, or widen it as you make the turn.

Experiment also with your entry into the turn by changing your angle of attack. You will find that turning early puts you on an arc that carries you wide as you come out of the turn, whereas entering the turn later puts you on a narrower exit arc (see Figure 2.3). Get comfortable with those cornering lines because you will find yourself using both in your races. Sometimes you'll be cornering solo and will have your choice of lines, and sometimes the presence of other riders in the turn will force a line on you. You will also find yourself in a race turning from a five-lane highway onto a roadway as narrow as a golf-cart path. You have to be comfortable with all scenarios.

Another visual that may help you appreciate what tires, wheels, bikes, and racers can do is to watch the pros go through a turn at superfast speeds and know that you're riding the exact same equipment. It's our own self-imposed limits, not the equipment, that prevent us from cruising through a turn so fast.

Eventually you will look at corners as nothing more than straight sections of road that aren't straight.

And yes, that's exactly what I meant to say.

When Cornering Goes Awry

The effects of centrifugal force can help you or hurt you, depending on your position in the pack. Knowing how momentum pushes bodies in motion to the outside of a turn, you can predict how it will affect your path of travel. You can therefore predict that any crash that occurs in a corner is going to sweep away from the apex. Therefore, if you're trying to avoid crashing, you should position yourself on the inside of the corner whenever possible. On a four-corner criterium course, this is relatively easy to do. But on a course with left and right turns, you may have trouble moving to the other side of the pack.

Riding on the outside of the pack as it negotiates a turn doesn't mean that you're in a bad spot. You simply need to keep your eyes open for riders in front of and beside you to be carried farther toward the outside. Don't be surprised by it. It's a law of physics that you can't change by writing to your senator.

DRINKING AND EATING

You may laugh, but fishing a bite to eat out of a back pocket or grabbing a water bottle is tricky for some people. Like all other skills, it must be mastered.

You will definitely need to drink something in every race you enter. If you need to pull over to the side of the road to do so, feel free. We'll wait for you at the car, which is parked just beyond the finish line.

You must be able to unwrap your food without swerving into the rider next to you. You must also be able to pull out your water bottle, drink from it, and replace it without taking out half the field.

While you're at it, you should be able to swap your water bottles in their cages. In other words, move one bottle to the front cage while moving the other to the back. Riders usually do this so that their full bottle is on the downtube and their empty bottle is on the seat tube. It shouldn't really matter because you should be able to grab either one from either cage and drink from it. But however you place your bottles, other racers want you to do it safely and expeditiously while following the contours of the course. That means that you need to be able to do it as you're going through a turn.

Watch out for the World War II cannon.

Eating on the bike may seem elementary. I'm sure you probably eat and drink while you're on a training ride, but it's a different ball game when you're elbow to elbow with a pack of riders who are trying to beat you. During a race, you're at the mercy of the pack. If they're hammering, you can forget table manners, but you can't forget to eat.

Here's a tip that comes from one of America's more successful cycling coaches of the 1980s, Mike Walden: Chew your food. Food that is pulverized in the mouth will be absorbed and digested more fully by the stomach. Therefore, the nutrients will be absorbed more quickly.

Another benefit of taking smaller bites and chewing your food thoroughly is that you will be less likely to choke on it while you're riding.

In the heat of a bike race, the tendency is to just get the food down as quickly as possible; there's no time to chew. Try not to do that. Make time. If all you have in your pocket is one nutrition bar, you will want to get as much out of it as possible, and proper digestion starts in your mouth. Pick a moment in the race that will allow you time to do this. Don't try to eat when the pack is strung out in single file. Don't eat during a climb; it'll block your breathing when you need it most. And, of course, remember the adage: Eat before you're hungry; drink before you're thirsty.

Just a little food for thought, and thought for food.

LOOKING OVER YOUR SHOULDER

Looking behind you sounds easy, doesn't it? I mean, we do it all the time when we ride. We look over our shoulders to spot cars approaching from the rear. The key to doing it in a bike race, however, is to be able to look over your shoulder without running into the riders next to you. If you do, you may discover the spokes of your front wheel getting jiggy with the rear derailleur of another bike.

The best way to test yourself is to ride on the white line near the edge of the roadway. Watch what happens to your line when you look behind you. If you're able to stay on the white line, you are certainly in the minority.

Imagine that you're in a pack of riders riding closer than your bib number, and you need to look back to see if any of your teammates are left in the race.

Or you're looking for your sprinter as you approach the Red Kite. He was told to be on your wheel in the last 2 miles. Where is he? You need to be able to find him without taking anyone to the ground.

First, you should just glance quickly. You're not standing on top of Lookout Mountain retracing the steps of the Confederate troops as they marched toward Chattanooga. You're just looking for a jersey the same color as yours. A simple movement like this shouldn't cause a wreck.

The key is to keep a consistent pressure on your handlebar. As we learned with countersteering, a gentle push on one side will take you off your line. To minimize this effect, hold your handlebar as near to the stem as possible.

Here's another way to catch a quick glimpse at what's behind you: Look under your arm. This takes a bit of practice, but it's much more subtle. In the chess game that's rolling down the road, subtlety is a good trait.

For example, I can tell when a rider is about to go on the attack if he spins around to take a quick look to see who is nearby. In the world of high-stakes poker, this is called a "tell." So if you want to be sneaky about it, just peek back under your arm. You'll be able to see if anyone is moving forward, and you won't broadcast your intentions.

You can also use this technique when you're on your solo attack to see if anyone has come up to join you. Sitting up and turning around will rob you of speed. A quick glance under your arm will suffice. You're not trying to determine anything more than whether or not anyone has joined your attack. If you discover that someone has joined you, you may then harass them mercilessly to pull through and do their share of the work.

Side note: Learn what your teammates' front wheels and forks look like so that you can differentiate between friend and foe at a glance. It'll be very useful someday.

Yet another way to look behind you: On a criterium course in the Columbus, Ohio, neighborhood of Short North near a college whose name I forget,

Chris Horner   LOOKING OVER YOUR SHOULDER

Looking over your shoulder is one of the necessities of bike racing, and it's important even when you're just out on a weekend ride. One year, when I was racing at the Fitchburg Longsjo Classic in Massachusetts, my old teammate Henk Vogels was just ahead of the field as we were coming down one of the fastest and roughest descents in domestic bike racing. I was on the front of the field, and Henk was at the back of the break that was just about to be caught. He looked back for just a moment to see what the gap was, and when he did, he overlapped wheels with the rider in front of him, who also happened to be an old teammate of mine. They were two of the most experienced guys in the field that day, but that didn't help them. We were easily doing 55 mph when Henk hit the deck hard.

To this day, it is still one of the scariest crashes that I have witnessed in the sport. Henk slid across the road and ended up bouncing off the guardrail before coming to a stop. The crash brought all of the racing to a halt while the ambulance was called to pick him up and take him to the emergency room. After that experience, I can't stress enough the importance of knowing exactly what is coming up in front of you, both immediately and farther down the road, before you take the time to look back.

Often, while on training rides or in bike races, when I need to look back, I put my hand on the shoulder of the teammate or friend riding next to me. This technique allows me to look back as long as I need to while the rider I'm holding on to controls our driving. I become an extension of the other rider and can move with him as he moves. But I have to stress that this can only be done when the rider next to you is someone whom you have complete faith in so that you don't end up hitting the deck together. ◾

breakaway riders were using a large storefront window as a rearview mirror to check the progress of the field chasing them. Clever.

USING THE BRAKES

Two basic rules of pack riding are "no sudden moves" and "no unpredictable moves." Braking is just one of many ways to make a sudden and unwelcome move. An axiom that's been around a while says, "The less you use your brakes, the faster you go."

A friend of mine used to say, "I only use my brakes once: when I get back to the car."

Famous Italian sprinter Mario Cipollini said it better: "You brake, you lose."

Battle-hardened riders will actually let out a wail of displeasure when someone in the peloton does something so utterly thoughtless as to cause them to apply the brakes in a race.

Braking falls under the umbrella of bike-handling skills. Part of making your bike an extension of your body is knowing its braking power. Knowing how much pressure to apply to slow from 28 mph to 26 mph comes with time and practice.

I always enjoy letting another rider take my bike for a spin. Invariably they return with a comment about my brakes. They're too mushy, or they're too touchy; something's different about them. It's not that my brakes are tuned in any radical way; they're just different than the ones on your bike because your bike is what you're used to.

But your brakes must stop you. And you must know their capabilities.

It's also handy to know that you can slow your bike without touching your brakes simply by catching more air. For example, while going downhill in a single-file line, you may find yourself creeping up on the rider in front of you. This is caused by the addition of gravity to the effects of drafting. (In my case, it's aided by the fact that I'm usually 23 pounds overweight.) Hitting your brakes now could have disastrous effects on the riders behind you. It breaks the rule of "no sudden moves." But if you sit up and catch a little wind, you'll shave off a few miles per hour and match the speed of the rider in front of you. Or you can move out of the draft to the side, and the same result will occur.

There will be times when heavy braking is required. It's important to know how your bike behaves when you do so. You must also pay attention to what your body weight does to the effectiveness of the brakes. As you squeeze the brake levers, your momentum will create a transference of weight from rear to front, placing more braking power on your front wheel. You'll need to counter-act this transference by moving your weight back on the bike in order to avoid flying over the handlebar (Figure 2.4). Moving your weight backward is done by pushing the bike forward underneath you as you brake. It must become instinctive for you to throw your handlebar forward when braking hard. Another option is to quickly embrace the power of prayer for a soft landing.

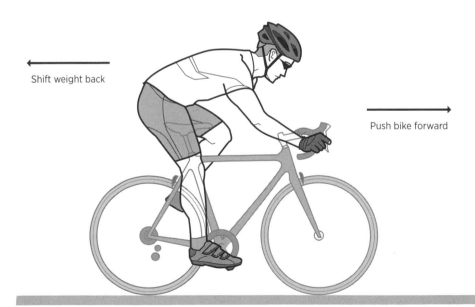

Shift weight back

Push bike forward

FIGURE 2.4 Counteract braking force by shifting your body weight back.

As for braking in the corners, don't make me warn you about the World War II cannon again.

Braking while cornering is tricky because of the same transference-of-weight phenomenon that I just discussed. Momentum is stubborn. You'll find that your bike's front wheel doesn't like being asked to do more than one thing at a time. You can ask it to corner, or you can ask it to brake, but you shouldn't ask it to do both at once. Give it a try, and you'll discover the limits of what your brakes and your bike can do in various states of change.

One more note about using the brakes: Never grab the levers. Instead, strive to always squeeze them progressively, even when you need to use the brakes hard. Practice squeezing the levers quickly but gently, and note the point at which the brake pads start to do their work. You want to be able to apply the brakes rapidly to this point and then continue to squeeze the levers as necessary to scrub off speed, or to stop completely if necessary. Grabbing the brake levers suddenly is a bad technique that you want to avoid; it can lead to an unstable bike, locked wheels, and a quick visit to the pavement, especially if you happen to be on a slippery surface.

DRAFTING

The most critical component of bike racing is drafting. It is your ticket to conserving your energy. It is what allows us all to race at high speeds without withering.

The draft is simply the absence of wind drag brought about by hiding behind another moving body. I can't overstate the importance of the ability to find and stay in the draft behind riders of every shape and size in winds from all directions. Drafting is more than a skill—it is a matter of survival in this sport.

The best nonbicycle example of drafting can be found in NASCAR racing, where we see cars lined up directly behind each other, taking advantage of the draft to travel at the same speed as the leader while using less energy. Note, however, that although this is a good visual example of drafting, it can be mis-leading for bike racing. New riders often assume that the draft is always located directly behind the rider in front of them because that's how it's portrayed at the Daytona 500. However, that's because those cars all have the same shape, and they're traveling at 180 mph. They're not fighting the effects of natural wind as much as the hurricane force created by their own speed. A 15 mph breeze doesn't cause a stock-car driver much worry, but it has a dramatic effect on a bike race.

In bike racing, the draft is much more varied (Figure 2.5). It is seldom located directly behind a rider. It can be found anywhere in the 180-degree arc behind him or her, depending on the wind direction, the wind speed, and the rider's speed.

Your job is to learn how to feel it. You must use your ears, the hair on your arms, and any other sensor you can think of to feel where the wind is and isn't. Understand that if you're feeling the wind, you're working harder than you need to. As I emphasized earlier, bike racing is a game of conservation.

FIGURE 2.5 Basic drafting positions

You need to learn to draft without (a) overlapping wheels and (b) repeatedly hitting the brakes. Overlapping wheels is a prelude to a crash as soon as the rider in front moves left or right more quickly than you can follow. That rider's back wheel will take out your front wheel, and down you will go. As for braking, you already know the first law of the pack: No sudden moves.

STANDING

This won't take long to explain. It's simple: Be careful when you stand on the pedals.

A moment ago, I explained the concept of throwing the bike out in front of you to avoid going over the handlebar as you brake hard. That same throwing motion will come in handy while sprinting. In a very close sprint, you may need to gain just a few inches over your competition as you cross the finish line. Track and field runners thrust their chests out to break the tape. Speed skaters thrust one foot ahead of them to break the electronic eye. Bike racers throw the bike forward to get the front wheel across the line first.

Bike throwing is a skill that, in reality, you may never use in your entire career. Still, it's a good move to have in your bag of tricks. It is accomplished by thrusting the bike forward at precisely the right moment to extend your reach over the finish line.

However, the exact opposite of this motion is what I call the "bike pull," and it usually occurs when you get out of the saddle during a climb. To quickly change positions from sitting to standing, you will actually pull the bike under you very abruptly. With this lightning-quick move, you will probably scare the crap out of the rider behind you because, although you think you're moving forward with your bike as one unit, you are actually causing your bike to nearly stop ever so briefly. The freaked-out rider behind you will see your rear wheel coming backward into the front wheel of his or her bike.

If you're the trailing rider, anticipate it and get over it. It happens all the time.

If you're the offending rider riding in a tightly bunched pack, try to stand up smoothly without jerking the bike backward.

If you're riding on your own, who cares? But even when you're riding on your own, you can practice being smoother.

STRETCHING

Debates rage among participants of all sports as to the benefit or detriment of pre-exercise stretching. Some believe it helps; others argue that it hinders performance. The debate gets heated at times.

That's funny because throughout my cycling career, I have almost never seen cyclists stretch before a ride. It's as if the idea never occurred to anyone in the sport.

Where cyclists do stretch, though, is on the bike after about the 30-mile point of a road race.

You can tell that riders are one with their bicycles when they can stretch their quads at 30 mph without wobbling. I've seen pro riders do this, and it's always impressive, but it's not a skill that's reserved only for that level of ability. Anyone can and should learn this.

> You can tell that riders are one with their bicycles when they can stretch their quads at 30 mph without wobbling.

Road races are long. The body aches. You can milk more miles out of your body by stretching your muscles during the race. How you do it is up to you, but you must be safe about it. I like to see riders drop to the back of the pack to work the kinks out. Stretching while you're on the front is considered bad form.

Stretching the calves is easy. You just have to put your foot at the bottom of the pedal stroke, drop your heel as far as you can, and lean forward slightly. You'll feel it.

You can stretch your lower back muscles by getting out of the saddle (smoothly, now that you've practiced), twisting your torso in both directions, and raising your shoulders. Some riders will stretch their quads by unclipping a foot from the pedal and pulling it up behind their butt. One hand stays on the bars; one foot stays clipped into the pedal.

I'm going to advise you to try this for the first time while riding on an indoor trainer with the front fork locked to a fork stand. I also urge you to make sure your cleats and pedals are in good shape. Because you'll be putting your weight onto one pedal at an odd angle, you don't want your cleat to disengage when you have one foot up behind your ear. That would get ugly. It sure sounds ugly the way I just described it.

At some point in your lifetime, you will likely experience severe leg cramps while riding. Rather than let them end your race day, you will need to find a way to fight through them so that you can complete the race. Stretching will help.

A few years ago, during a long, hilly road race in Ohio, I experienced severe cramps in my inner thighs with only 10 miles left in the race. Horribly pain-ful—it felt like iron bands had been tightened around my legs. I dropped like a stone to the back of the pack and considered dropping out altogether. I had been riding well until then, so I decided to work it out. The only relief I could find was to drag my inner thighs repeatedly across the top tube of my bike with as much force as I could. I'm sure it was a strange sight to anyone who hap-pened to be watching. But it worked, and I was able to finish the race in 11th place. Unfortunately, the prize list paid to 10.

Start small during your next solo ride, on the trainer.

SHIFTING/GEARING

Here's yet another topic that should be obvious to anyone who has ever ridden a bike with more than one gear: Smooth shifting is a good skill to have. It's included in that "bike/extension/body" idea that I presented earlier. You don't want to botch a shift or drop a chain at the wrong moment in a race. Missing a shift when the heat is on can cause you to lose several places in a short amount of time. You will also want to know how to remount the chain should it fall off the chainrings, and you'll want to do that without pulling over to the side of the road and getting off the bike.

Obviously, the best way to remount a chain is to buy an entirely new, fully assembled bike in your favorite color. This is a foolproof method, but time-consuming and expensive. A more practical technique is to shift the front derailleur to push the chain back up onto the chainring while pedaling very slowly.

If you can't get the chain back onto the ring by using the shifter, don't try to use your hands while riding. That technique has "hospital visit" written all over it. Instead, you'll have to stop, dismount, reach in and grab the chain with your hand, and place it on the ring. Take your time and get it done on the first try. Don't lose more time through frustration.

In a criterium, where allowances are made for mechanical failures, a dropped chain does not qualify as "mechanical." It is considered to be operator error, so you won't be granted a "free lap." You must come to the starting line with a fully working bicycle.

Part of knowing gears and shifting is knowing how to adjust and fine-tune the parts yourself. You may think that I'm speaking to only about 4 percent of the cycling world with that comment, but you'd be shocked to know how many roadies don't really know how to adjust the derailleurs on their bikes. According to bike shops that I polled, the percentage is close to 40 percent. For the other 60 percent, it's just part of bike ownership to understand how it works and how to fix it when it doesn't.

Gearing may never come up in conversation at dinner parties, but it's handy when figuring out distances and cadences. You'll be more hip among cyclists if you speak in "gear inches," and you'll be able to figure out your ideal sprinting gear and make adjustments when you convert it to inches.

"Gear inches" refers to the distance (in inches) that the bike will travel in one full revolution of the pedals in a given gear. For instance, if the chain is on the biggest chainring in the front and the littlest cog in the back, that is considered the "biggest" gear on the bike because you're covering the greatest distance with each pedal stroke. For a bike with a 53-11 gearing, for example, that's about 127 inches of roadway. So when a cyclist tells you to use a "smaller gear," they want you to shift to a gear that's easier to pedal.

The Gear Chart on page 256 shows the gear inches for every combination found on the standard road bike. I promise you that bicycle nerds pore over these numbers with the same vigor that I pore over the dessert menu at my favorite restaurant. And I can recite the menu by heart.

3

PACK RIDING AND OTHER SKILLS

ONE THING THAT SETS BIKE RACING APART from almost every other sport—and takes spectators' breath away—is how close the pack rides together. It is truly amazing to see a dense group of 150 riders wind their way across the landscape mere inches from each other. It's a thing of beauty when a peloton moves like a school of fish through a tight corner.

Of course, if you are not comfortable riding wheel to wheel, sitting in the pack can also be unnerving and dangerous. Worrying about riding so close might be a key reason why many racers wash out of the sport. To some, it feels as if a crash is imminent at all times, no matter what the speed.

Riding in that beautiful school of fish requires skills that you won't find in most other sports. But you can learn those skills—obviously, as we would have no peloton otherwise.

So, the race begins. Right from the gun, there is a fight for position. Every bike racer knows that the racing takes place at the front of the pack, and everyone knows that the road is only wide enough to handle so many bodies. We also know that crashes happen everywhere within the peloton, but our odds of avoiding a crash are better near the front. Therefore, the first burst is going to be intense as everyone tries to be among the top 20 places.

The general rule is: The shorter the race, the more intense the first miles will be. A corollary to that rule is: The more technical and challenging the course, the more intense the first bit will be. So if the race is 120 miles long, you can expect a mellow start. However, if there's a tough hill in the first few miles, you can expect a mad dash to be near the front. If the race is a criterium held on a very technical course, expect a volcanic eruption off the line.

In any case, you will immediately find yourself elbow to elbow and wheel to wheel with everyone else. Are you ready for this? I hope so. Add pack-riding skills to the growing list of "must haves." Training rides usually follow orderly pacelines, both single and double. Bike races are a bit more random. Pack riding means you must find the draft, fight for position, and avoid crashing.

HOLDING A STEADY SPEED

Riders in a pack want predictability in their compatriots. If you can't hold a steady speed, you will annoy the entire peloton. If you can't ride a straight line, you will imperil it. The phrase that cyclists use to describe all-over-the-place riding is "squirrelly." I think it comes from what we all imagine a real squirrel would do on a bike (if it could reach the pedals). A squirrel is a nervous, fidgety, frenetic creature that would create havoc in a bike race.

Steady and straight are fundamental skills that all new riders must learn whether they race or not. And in a race, riders near you will demand those skills. They are safety issues. And depending on how unstraight your line is and at which point in a race you are, you may be penalized. For example, USAC rules state that no rider may make an abrupt motion that might interfere with the forward progress of another rider.

The rules say nothing about slowly weaving down the road singing "O Sole Mio" at the top of your lungs. As long as your motion is not abrupt and a hindrance to others and your singing isn't horrible, we'll let it slide. But if you are a threat to the forward progress and well-being of others, we will get vocal very quickly. We may even yell.

One cause of twitchy riding is gripping the handlebar too tightly. If you hold on with a death grip, the bike will react to every impulse you send through your arms. Just think of your grandfather's handshake: soft and gentle, but you know he isn't letting go. Work on that. And learn to trust the gyroscopic effect of the front wheel to keep you on track. To do so, you must remove the tension from your hands, arms, and shoulders and let the bike flow while you smoothly apply power with your legs. Think of yourself as a cruise ship: Everyone's relaxed and having a great time going with the flow up on the lido deck while the real work is done down in the engine room to drive the boat forward.

> *Learn to trust the gyroscopic effect of the front wheel to keep you on track.*

Another cause of twitchiness is reacting to every movement that happens near you. This usually stems from looking at the rider directly in front of you instead of looking farther ahead at the whole of the pack. I'll talk more about this when I cover pack-riding skills a little later. For now, understand that your reactions to the little movements around you are costing you energy and making you unpredictable, which in turn makes everyone around you nervous.

Twitchiness can refer to your random side-to-side motions, but it is also reflected in your front-to-back motion or fluctuating speed. If your speed varies by just 1 mile per hour, it's still a variation, and if it varies constantly, it will create problems for riders behind you. If the rider behind you is an opponent, he or she will not enjoy it. If the rider behind you is a teammate, he or she will not enjoy it, either.

Riding at a varying speed will also slowly leak energy out of you. You won't feel the energy slip away because it will happen over the course of several miles.

You also won't feel that you're slowing down and speeding up because you've probably always done this; you may not yet know what steady speed feels like.

You won't spot this fluctuation on a speedometer. The speed variation that I'm talking about happens at a microlevel. It looks something like this: two quick pedal strokes followed by two slower pedal strokes, followed by coasting, followed by three very fast pedal strokes, followed by one easy pedal stroke, followed by a stick thrust into your spokes by the guy who was behind you.

If you drove your car like that, you would get horrible gas mileage and no one would want to ride in the car with you. So don't ride like that on your bike.

BUMPING OTHERS

If you get nervous and twitchy when riders move near you, you're not ready for what we're going to cover next: physical contact.

I attended a workshop at the Olympic Training Center in Colorado Springs a long time ago. I think it was in the late 1800s. I traveled there by stagecoach. Everyone wore wool. Everyone got tangled in exposed brake cables. But the lessons are still valid today.

The camp was conducted by notable riders who had extensive palmarès (race results). We took our bikes to a nearby park and spent two hours running into each other. It was one of the most productive days in my racing career, and the skills I learned have served me well ever since. Here is a list of drills that we accomplished at this simple workshop.

Tumbling and tuck-and-rolls on the grass. These rolls (conducted without the bike, obviously) are pretty basic, but they will teach you how not to use your hands, face, or head to break your fall. You can find them in any gymnastics book.

Side-by-side riding with contact. Pair up with a partner and ride side by side with your hands on the drops, making contact with your elbows.

In my class, we at first made contact at the elbows, but we became more brazen with each attempt until finally we were literally bashing into each other without falling over. I'm not kidding.

Later we tried to lean over and push our partners off their bikes using a shoulder. Each time we increased our speed a bit. Eventually we were able to do this at a decent clip. In time we were doing this at race pace on pavement.

It sounds completely wrong, doesn't it? Granted, it's against the rules to make contact like this intentionally during a race, but there will be times when you suddenly find yourself bumping shoulders with your neighbors. Get used to how it feels.

Wheel tapping. With everyone closely following one another on a grassy area, repeatedly tap the rear wheel ahead with your front wheel. The object is to gain empirical confidence that wheel-to-wheel contact won't kill you, and the key, as usual, is to remain relaxed.

Slalom forward. Start in a single file line with at least one bike length between riders. The last one rides forward to the front of the line by weaving back and forth as if each rider is an orange traffic cone. The next rider follows the advancing rider to the front, where they then become traffic cones for the other riders. This teaches advancing riders to move forward through a pack, and it teaches those riding as traffic cones to get comfortable with riders squeezing through gaps.

Up the alley. Two single-file lines ride fairly close together at a steady speed. The last rider in line rides up through the middle. You can vary the width of the alley to suit the abilities of your riders. It won't be long before you're bumping elbows and hips all the way up to the front. It's also fun to call each other names and threaten to burn the advancing riders' villages to the ground. Here's a tip for completing the drill successfully: Pillage first. Then burn.

Chop. This one requires a beater bike. Use your water bottles to stake out an area large enough to contain your group of riders with enough room to move about. Quite simply, the last rider standing is declared the winner. You are free to make as much contact as you feel comfortable making. You must keep your hands on the drops at all times. Good luck.

//

We crashed several times while we conducted most of these drills, but we fell onto soft grass at slow speeds. And since we had learned how to crash and tumble properly earlier in the day, we all survived quite nicely, and I have the grass stains to prove it.

These are valuable drills to work on periodically with your own clubmates. You will become a better rider immediately. The drills will teach you how to relax and absorb contact. You will gain confidence and lose fear—two things as important as speed and power.

Don't use your good bike for these exercises; use your rain bike or beater bike. You can wear pads if you wish. Do whatever it takes for you to feel comfortable bumping into other riders, but do it. It's going to happen to you during a race, and you don't want to freak out when it does.

PACELINES AND ROTATING PACELINES

The paceline is one of my favorite sporting experiences. It is as important to cycling tactics as a drum roll is to a marching band playing "The Star-Spangled Banner." I suppose you could play the song without it, but no one ever does.

Pacelines are created to share the workload among two or more riders. A paceline is what allows a group of riders to ride faster than any one of them could alone. Bike racers simply must know the mechanics of a paceline, just as every center fielder in baseball must know how to stand in a meadow for hours at a time.

If you don't know how a paceline works, here's an absurd but accurate lesson: Let's say that you're watching the Miss America Pageant on TV. A steady stream of contestants walks out on stage. One at a time and evenly spaced, they walk toward the camera, smile, and recite their name and the state they represent. They then peel off and go find their place on the risers, where they wait for the rest to join them.

Let's pretend that instead of finding their spot on the risers, they go backstage to the end of the line and shuffle through it again and again. Each time they come to the front, they pause just long enough to deliver their lines before peeling off.

That, my friends, is a paceline. And yours should be so graceful.

What's different in cycling, of course, is the purpose of that line. You are hiding from the wind—drafting—except for the brief moment when you're at the front of the line giving your name and the state you represent.

When the rider on the front decides that he's had enough, he pulls to the side and goes back to the end of the line (Figure 3.1). When he reaches the end of the line, he accelerates to match the speed and get back into the draft. He then follows the rider in front of him to the front of the line again.

He can stay on the front as long as he wishes. It's really up to him. He can stay there long enough to say, "I'm Bruce. I'm from Indiana!" Or if he's really ambitious, he can stay up there long enough to say, "I'm Bruce. I'm originally

FIGURE 3.1 Single paceline

from Indiana, but now I live in New York. I went to college in Chicago and thought I'd stay for grad school, but it didn't work out. . . ." We just ask—insist, really—that he keep the tempo steady and the effort constant. While he's up there, he is working harder than everyone else. If he wants to stay there all day, that's fine with me. I'm drafting. And I'm sorry grad school didn't work out. Tell me more.

When he does pull aside, he must do so on the windward side of the paceline. That is, into the wind (Figure 3.2). This is a cardinal rule of cycling. To break the rule could cause a crash. At the very least, it will invite howls of derision from the other riders.

Once he pulls off, he is free to decide how long he should take to find the back of the line. He should know that he is expending energy as he does so. If he drops too slowly, he'll waste energy riding unprotected in the wind. If he drops too quickly, he'll have to accelerate harder to match the speed of the line as it passes him. Timing the retreat is a skill that takes time to master.

That is an ordinary paceline.

The next level of difficulty is the rotating paceline.

In an ordinary paceline, you follow the leader forward. When the leader peels off, you take your turn on the front. You then peel off and drop back to the

FIGURE 3.2 Pull off into the wind.

FIGURE 3.3 Rotating paceline

end of the line at your own pace. In a rotating paceline, you follow the leader to the front, but when you drop to the back of the line, you draft off the next contestant as he drops backward (Figure 3.3). As a result, you are protected in both lines: advancing and retreating. It's brilliant.

This time the rider on the front cannot decide for himself how long he wants to stay on the front or how long he wants to take to go to the back. Each rider must perform these actions in the same rhythm. As soon as the rider gets to the front, he will smoothly pull aside and begin his retreat. There is no such thing as free will in a rotating paceline.

Just like the Miss America Pageant, the paceline needs to work like clock work. There can't be gaps in the line. You all have to move at the same speed when advancing, and a slightly slower but uniform speed when retreating. And just like the Miss America contestants, you need to be careful not to cause a crash that takes down several others in the process. Rest assured that Miss Pennsylvania has that exact same fear.

The key to success is your ability to ride close to the rider in front of you and to do so steadily. Also key is your ability to find the draft, stay in the draft, and use the draft to protect you whether you're advancing in one line or retreating in the other.

Pacelines are where we find the best example of synergy: You will go faster in a group than you would individually. The rotating paceline relies on the cooperation of everyone involved. Consequently, it doesn't take much to mess it up. In a bike race, you need to know both ends of that spectrum: how to make it work smoothly and how to make it not work at all, as you would do if you had a teammate off the front whose position you wanted to protect.

Where a paceline usually breaks down is when riders cause speeds to fluctuate. Accelerating when taking over the lead position is a common mistake. Retreating too quickly or too slowly will make a mess of the paceline (Figure 3.4). Riders must make a smooth transition between the advancing lane and the retreating lane and not allow gaps to open up between riders. For instance, if Miss Ohio gets lost on her way to the back of the line, it will cause confusion for the rest of the contestants. Maybe Miss Ohio does this on purpose in order to create drama. Perhaps Miss Ohio wants to throw things out of whack to prevent Miss Michigan from winning. It all depends on Miss Ohio's motivation. We will explore such mischievous intentions later on when we discuss breakaways and blocking.

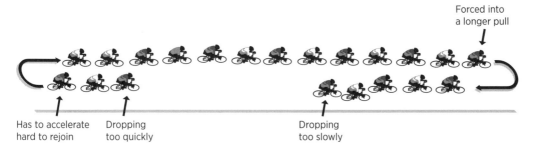

FIGURE 3.4 Dropping too slowly or too quickly creates gaps. Gaps are bad.

Plugging Gaps

If gaps open in a rotating paceline, you must determine why they are happening. Is someone trying to mess up the rhythm? Or has someone simply blown up and can no longer keep pace? In either case, if you don't fix the problem, the paceline may fall apart.

Here are two common scenarios and ways to fix them.

The second rider in the advancing line reaches the front and accelerates too hard. (This is all too common.) The next rider can't match the pace. When a gap opens between the leader and the rest of the line, the second rider is faced with a choice. He can accelerate and try to catch the leader, or he can simply forget about the leader and rotate as usual when he has room to move to the retreating line. In my opinion, the latter option is best, as it's less disruptive to the rhythm.

At the back of the line, a rider misses the transition from the retreating line to the advancing line. He waits too long to accelerate. As a result, a gap opens in the advancing line. That rider will now face a headwind as he proceeds to the front of the line, or he can shout out to the riders in the retreating line to fill the gap in front of him. Here, I like the second option because it maintains a full advancing line. Gaps in the retreating line aren't as crucial as gaps in the advancing line.

//

One thing that helps the rotation is to be vocal when you're transitioning into the advancing line. Let the rider in front of you know that you're the last in line so that he's not taken by surprise when you pass him. It doesn't matter what you say as long as it gets the message across. Don't say, "Hey, look over there!"

This little heads-up is particularly important when riders start dropping out of the line because it's going too fast for them, or because they are leaving to take their kid to a dental appointment. When riders start disappearing off the back, the end of the line comes sooner than expected. Heads up.

Hills and Descents

Another situation that breaks up a rotating paceline is a hill. We have a general rule for this: Maintain steady effort, not steady speed. It's natural to let your speed dip as the road begins to rise. If you try to maintain the same speed, you'll strain the weaker riders in the paceline, and gaps will open. Similarly, don't try to rotate at the same pace as on flat terrain. That speed will drop in relation to the pace of the line.

On steep hills that require a lot of effort, the effects of drafting are insignificant, so rotating is unnecessary. Therefore, suspend the rotation until you get over the hill. When you get over the crest, pick up where you left off.

On descents, the group will likely descend at the same relative speed, so rotation is unnecessary. However, the riders on the front of both the advancing and the retreating line must continue to pedal. They must never coast down the hill while on the front of a paceline. They are fighting wind resistance while everyone behind them is not. As a result, the trailing riders will be sucked into the backs of the riders in front of them. No one enjoys this.

The rotating paceline is pure magic when it works properly. I hope you'll take a moment to enjoy the clocklike precision of a good rotation when it comes.

And just when you think cycling can't get any cooler, the wind changes direction and something happens to that paceline. It echelons.

ECHELONS

An echelon is simply a diagonal paceline. Echelons run at an angle because the wind is coming from an angle rather than head-on (Figure 3.5). When the wind does this, the draft isn't found immediately behind a rider; it's off to one side. Thus, the diagonal line. Apart from this, the same rules of rotation apply.

Basic Echelon

The echelon formation is not announced at the beginning of a ride. There is no proclamation made: "On my command, fellow riders, begin the echelon formation!" It just happens when the wind dictates. You need to know how.

FIGURE 3.5 Single echelon

FIGURE 3.6 The line doesn't have to be straight; the riders just need to be in the draft.

My problem with echelons is that they're always portrayed in bike racing literature as a straight line angling from left to right (or right to left) at about 45 degrees. Each rider is drawn in perfect alignment with the next, and the wind is drawn as a straight line coming from the side, or perhaps from a 45-degree angle.

In reality, it's never that perfect. Riders who try to stick to the precision of an illustration will be frustrated by the experience. Oftentimes I see ride leaders or instructors fixating on the straightness of a paceline or the correct angle of an echelon. They'll shout at riders to keep the line straight when, in actuality, it doesn't make any difference. As long as you feel the draft and derive the golden benefits of being in the draft, you're in the right position (Figure 3.6).

FIGURE 3.7 If you can't find the draft, you'll stick out like a sore thumb.

This is not marching band. We're not trying to spell a word. In this formation, the most we could muster is a backslash, which might come in handy if we were performing a halftime tribute to the URL.

The wind is seldom steady in speed and direction, so the location of the draft is constantly changing (Figure 3.7). As a result, each rider makes continual microadjustments to stay protected. As such, the paceline waves with every small change of wind direction.

To practice an echelon, you need some wind. Without it, the paceline's forward progress creates its own breeze, and the draft is found immediately behind each rider, thus creating a straight line from front to back. When wind is present, however, the location of the draft changes with each bend in the road, and the angle of the paceline changes, too. That's why it's impossible to practice an echelon while riding on a calm day.

The nuance involved in a rotating echelon is incredible. A lot of things must come together to make it work properly. Not only are you concerned with saving your own energy, but you're also concerned with preserving the cohesiveness of the line in order to milk as much speed as possible from the group. On top of that, you must consider the safety of everyone involved. Even Miss Ohio, who we suspect wants to mess up the cohesiveness, has no interest in crashing.

Chris Horner   MY FIRST EUROPEAN ECHELON

My first experience with a European echelon came in 1997, when I was riding with the Française des Jeux team. In the U.S., the echelon is almost nonexistent. In all my years of racing before heading to Europe, I could only recall one time in which the echelon had had any impact on a race whatsoever. But at that time, I was so strong that riding in the front echelon wasn't a problem for me; it was simply a matter of using more energy to be at the front when I needed to be. When I hit Europe in 1997, though, I was facing a field of a whole different quality.

I was racing one of the French cup races in northern France, where the wind blows from the side more often than in any other place in the world. I was on the tail end of the front echelon, all the way in the left gutter, suffering on the limit and not getting much of the draft since I clearly wasn't actually in the echelon. When I really started suffering, I immediately started thinking, "Start the second echelon, Chris." It was something I had always been told but had never needed before this moment. I swung hard to the right side of the road to start the second echelon, but when I looked to my left to see how many guys I had with me, I realized there was nobody on my wheel. The real second echelon had started well before that point and was at least 400 meters behind me.

That would be the first lesson I learned that day: Make sure there's actually someone on your wheel before you start the next echelon! I learned the second lesson on that very same stretch of road only a few moments later: When the next echelon arrives, if the wind is coming from

→

MY FIRST EUROPEAN ECHELON, CONTINUED

the right to the left, you'd better be on the left. At the time, I thought it was a great idea to stay on the right—right up until the second echelon went past me so fast that I wasn't even able to think about getting back in the group. Unfortunately, within just a few moments, I had learned two valuable echelon lessons!

As the third echelon arrived, I remembered my first two lessons very well and stayed on the left side of the road, but not all the way in the gutter. I positioned myself so that when the echelon reached me, it had no choice but to let me in—that or run me over. Before I knew it, I was back in the group, rotating in the echelon, and hoping that we would meet back up with the first and second groups, which of course never happened because the wind never stopped blowing. But with a couple of valuable lessons learned, the day was not a total failure when I finally crossed the finish line, far behind the day's winner. ◾

Advanced Echelon

There are actually two different types of rotating echelon pacelines. They are made different by the severity of the angle of wind. If the wind is coming from the front at an angle between, say, the eleven o'clock and one o'clock positions, the paceline will simply cant to the appropriate angle (see Figure 3.5). This makes rotating a little trickier, as riders are now advancing and retreating in an oblique formation. Much more care must be taken to not create gaps and to not overlap wheels.

If, however, the wind is coming from a more dramatic angle—say, straight from the side at the three o'clock or nine o'clock position—the echelon may morph into one that is more diagonal (Figure 3.8). We see this frequently in European races during the spring classics, which are held on wide-open country roads. It is very different from a double paceline in that each rider is drafting someone who is almost next to him instead of in front of him. This is a much more advanced technique for hiding from the wind. It requires more attention from the riders, as they are moving sideways to rotate in a line while that line is moving straight ahead. It can get confusing.

FIGURE 3.8 The paceline becomes oblique in the wind.

Also, because of the steeper angle, this type of echeloning paceline will quickly spread across the roadway. Sadly, the road is only wide enough for so many bodies. This leaves some riders out in the wind struggling to find a draft as they hug the very edge of the pavement (Figure 3.9). They will derive no benefit of the draft and must try to form a secondary echelon behind the lead echelon.

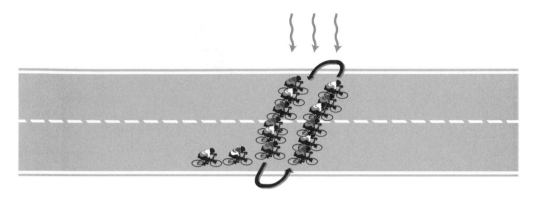

FIGURE 3.9 Diagonal echelon: When the wind comes straight from the side, riders shelter next to each other. There's often not enough rooom for everybody.

You can use this situation to your advantage. If you want to splinter the group and create havoc for the rest of the field (which should be your intention at all times), your team can limit the number of riders in the first echelon by placing the front of it in such a position in the lane that it only allows a certain number of riders to benefit. For example, if the front rider is on the yellow line at the center of the road, the echelon will only be long enough for eight or nine riders to benefit. The rest of the field will be forced to string out in a single-file line in the right gutter (the edge of pavement, that is; cyclists like to use the word "gutter" because it sounds more menacing). If second and third echelons form, gaps will naturally open between the echelons. At that point, the race becomes a pursuit among the different groups.

Someday you will race on a day when the wind is ferocious. If you're comfortable with the rotating double-echelon paceline with a lemon spritzer, you'll do just fine.

I attended college in a town that is surrounded by farmland, much like the countryside in Belgium. The wind blew hard across the landscape

Chris Horner MY SECOND EUROPEAN ECHELON

My second big echelon experience was during the 1998 Grand Prix du Midi Libre stage race. I was still riding for the French team Française des Jeux, and Midi Libre would finish about five weeks before the Tour de France began. I was riding extremely well and was sitting solidly in the top 10 before the last stage began. That morning I was told for the first time in my cycling career that I would be doing the Tour de France. You can't imagine how excited and happy I was all morning, waiting for the last stage to begin and looking forward to an unbelievable summer of racing.

The final stage started with intense racing immediately. The front group was about 30 miles from the finish when we once again were in a strong crosswind section. Within a few moments, the Festina team and I were the only ones left in the front echelon. On this particular section, the road was very narrow and lined with trees, just as you see in all the picture-perfect postcards from France. One major problem with an echelon, though, is that if one rider is dodging a hole or other obstacle in the road, his movements to the right or left create a wave effect down the group that intensifies with each rider and threatens to send the last guy off the road if he runs out of real estate.

Shortly after the front echelon had been established, one of the big stars on Française des Jeux, Evgeni Berzin, a past winner of the Giro d'Italia and Liège–Bastogne–Liège, was able to jump from the second echelon to the first echelon, where of course I was. I immediately saw him and moved as far to the left side of the road as possible to make a place for him to come into the echelon. This caused one big problem, though: With each

→

MY SECOND EUROPEAN ECHELON, CONTINUED

sway in the group, I was left with zero room to navigate. Right then one of the Festina guys suddenly swerved heavily, sending a ripple through our group. At that moment I had two options: (1) go off the road and into the gravel, possibly hitting one of the thousands of trees lining the road, or (2) run into my teammate, whom I had just let into the group. I chose to hit my teammate instead of the tree, thinking that it gave me the best chance of coming out of the crash in one piece. After I hit the ground, I picked up my bike and got back onto my teammates' wheels; they were all waiting to take me back to the front of the race. As soon as I stood up out of the saddle to accelerate for the first time, I realized that the echelon had had no mercy. The crash had broken my wrist and in less than a day's time had destroyed my hopes of making the Tour de France team. ◼

because, frankly, there wasn't much there to stop it. I remember some windy days in which I was drafting a rider whose left knee was bumping my right handlebar.

If that's where the draft is, that's where you'll find me.

PACK RIDING IN THE WIND

There's more to pack riding than just riding along in a blob. You must know what the wind is doing and how it will affect the shape of that blob. You must have an invisible wind gauge on your nose that tells you when you're fighting the wind and when you're not. Wind equals exertion, equals tired, equals not winning prize money. As riders move about you, as the pack changes direction and the wind shifts, you must read your internal wind gauge more often than a pilot checks his altimeter and much more often than the Titanic watchmen checked for icebergs.

At first glance, the peloton appears to be an amorphous shape of randomly placed riders, but there is often a defined order in which riders form pacelines within the group. The lines are not rotating, nor are they straight. They are simply formed organically as riders attempt to hide from the wind. You may have four or five ribbons of riders lined up next to each other, each one waving like a flag reacting to the many changes in wind direction. When two lines drift apart slightly, the wind will fill the void between them. If your nose is alone in that alleyway, you will be riding in a chute of wind (Figure 3.10). But because you're in the middle of the peloton, you may think that you're protected. The red light on your internal wind gauge should be lit up like a beacon, but you may fail to notice it. You're pushing big wind, and you're burning matches in the process. Get out of that chute.

You'll see this happen often in the lower categories. Unfamiliar with the physics of wind, newer riders will dutifully follow the written rule of hiding in a peloton, but they will ignore the more defined rule of hiding behind someone in the peloton. There's a big difference between the two.

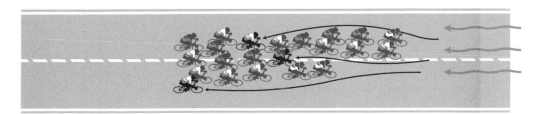

FIGURE 3.10 Pack riding into the wind; beware of wind chutes.

Another place to find wind while riding in the peloton is on the windward side of the group. Remembering the valuable lessons of an echelon will help you find the leeward side of the pack and therefore the easier place to ride.

SEEING MOVEMENTS

It's been said that when a butterfly flaps its wings in the Amazon rainforest, it sets into motion a chain of events that can have consequences on the other side of the planet. So, too, in a bike race. A simple change in speed in one corner of the peloton can soon affect what's happening on the other side of the road. Seeing these simple shifts is a skill that good bike racers will develop over time. It's a skill that will come in handy in every race.

Some riders wait for things to happen and then react to them. Good riders see everything and anticipate what will happen.

For instance, a good rider notices when the right side of the field slows a little and knows what that will do to the left side of the field: The left side suddenly finds itself thrust to the front of the race. If there's a rider on the left side of the field who has been waiting to pounce, this may be his opportunity—which means it may be your opportunity, too.

While on the topic of pouncing riders, watch the way riders move forward toward the front of the pack. You can tell if they're moving up with the intention to attack or if they're simply moving up to be nearer to the front. Their body language, head movements, and cadence will be giveaways. If they're about to attack, they will accelerate as they near the front. They'll also be "on top of the gear," which means they won't be lumbering. They'll probably be in the drops (hands in the lower curve of the handlebar) with their weight shifted forward, ready to spring into attack mode. Conversely, a rider who is just moving forward will be on the hoods (hands on the brake hoods), keeping a steady speed.

Another movement to watch for is the sweeping side-to-side motion that we see, usually into a headwind, when the rider on the front wants to pull off and no one else wishes to take over the lead. Some riders make an exaggerated move to one side, baiting someone else to pull through. Instead, everyone follows, sweeping the entire field to the same side. It seems that the field is content to sit in this poor guy's draft all day. However, back in 20th position, there's one rider who has been waiting for an opportunity to launch his attack. When the lead riders appear to be reluctant to push forward, now may be the time. If the side movement opens up a hole, that rider may attack up the road. Be alert.

It's impossible to list all the movements that might occur during a race and what they might do to the complexion of a race. I can only stress the importance of watching all that's happening and understanding that when a metaphorical butterfly flaps its wings in the peloton, big changes can follow.

That is, if you're in the race to actually race. If you're just in the race to get some fast miles, you can ignore the signs and sit at the back watching for actual butterflies.

CLIMBING

In the American racing scene, there aren't many races that feature the seemingly endless, gut-busting climbs that we see in the European Grand Tours. The climbs that do exist here are notorious and are unlikely to sneak up on you. If you're a horrible climber, you probably won't sign up for a race on Mount Washington in New Hampshire, Independence Pass in Colorado, Mount Baldy in California, Brasstown Bald in Georgia, or Mount Mitchell in South Carolina. I've never raced up any of those. I know better.

Instead, you're more likely to tackle the hill on the backstretch of the criterium course in Nevada City, California, or the nasty climb at Snake Alley in Iowa.

Regardless of the size of the hills, you have to know how to go up them. To be a weak climber is a huge blind spot that will cost you dearly at some point.

You will eventually enter a race with a big hill on the course, and you will have to go up it. There's no getting around it, and you can't take the escalator.

There is no secret formula to being a good climber. The odds are in your favor if you're slight of build, but you can't use that as an excuse if you're a bigger rider. I know a lot of bigger riders who can gallop up a hill with ease. I'm not one of them. I'm also not one to lay down a law about how something is done. You should find your own style by experimenting with your weight distribution, gearing, cadence, tempo, and pedal stroke until you find the best combination.

There are riders who sit and spin a smallish gear and others who jump out of the saddle and push a big gear. There are those who move their weight forward and waggle their body and bike side to side. Some move their weight back. Others hold their bike and body rigid. A few get off and walk.

There's no right or wrong way. (Well, except walking.) It's going to take X amount of watts to get your body mass to the top of the hill whether you rely on spinning (using a small gear and high cadence) or mashing (large gear, slow cadence). Each will take its toll. You can decide which is best for your riding style.

Without question, the best place to grip the bars when riding out of the saddle is on the hoods.

Without question, the best position to grip the bars when riding out of the saddle is on the hoods. This provides the best leverage and the best breathing thanks to the wider spread of your arms. I sometimes see new riders holding on to the bars on the tops or at the bend. I know it's physically possible to do so, but there are problems with these positions. First, they don't allow you to reach the brake levers. Also, your grip is compromised because of the angle of your hands in relationship to the force.

Instead, imagine how you would pick up a heavy suitcase. That's the ideal angle to pull on the handlebars when climbing and sprinting, and that angle is with your hands wrapped around the hoods.

As the race approaches the climb, consider first things first: How big is the climb? How has it been raced in the past? Where does it come in the race? And where does the climb actually begin?

Some riders start climbing before they reach the real part of the climb. This usually means that the difficulty of the climb has gotten into their heads, and they're already giving in to it. They may be on a false flat leading up to the climb, but they've already begun the lumbering process. Don't imitate them. Wait until everyone around you starts to climb. That's where the climb starts.

One popular tactic that nonclimbers use is to begin the climb at the front of the group. This is a way to minimize their losses. If they begin the climb at the front, they can ride at their own tempo and allow several riders to pass them while still maintaining contact with the main bunch. That's the idea, anyway. If it's a decisive climb that comes at a strategic point in the race, it may be difficult to get to the front, as all the soon-to-be attackers are already amassing there. Still, the nonclimbers must do what they can.

Don't try to tackle the entire hill in one effort. Accept the fact that there will be slow parts, surges, and attacks. Respond to them only when they come. Not before.

If a particular hill has been used in a race before, then it has some sort of history that you can study beforehand. If it has a history of being an explosive climb, be ready for it.

If you're one of the would-be attackers who has waited for this moment to unleash doom upon the other riders, you must know your own abilities and attack at the moment that is right for you. Attack too early, and you'll fade before you reach the top. Attack too late, and you'll gain no advantage. If you don't attack at all, you'll have given up your strength.

One thing to keep in mind while climbing is that if the race doesn't end at the top of the hill, the world doesn't end if you get dropped. Don't panic. You may be able to get back into contention after the climb. Just keep the lead pack within reach. Don't put yourself into an anaerobic deficit, but instead pace yourself carefully so that you're able to work hard after the climb.

You know what lies ahead because you studied the course beforehand, right? Of course you did.

RECON THE COURSE

If you love surprises, roll up to the starting line without peeking at the course. Don't look at a map, profile, or hand-drawn etching. Don't talk to anyone. Just roll. You are sure to be surprised.

Meanwhile, the rest of the field will study the course. It's what every rider should do.

Of course, the ideal situation is not just to look at the course but to ride it in advance while paying close attention to hills, hazards, and the final 3 miles. If the race is a criterium, you may be able to sneak a quick lap between races when one field is cooling down and the next field is warming up. By riding it, you can actually pace off the last 200 meters, check the pavement, test the cornerability of the turns, and note the tricky features. (Two hundred meters is the benchmark distance that sprinters use to time their sprint. The last 200 meters is usually demarcated by an orange cone or a sign. We'll discuss this magic number later when we cover sprinting.)

Sometimes, however, a criterium's schedule will be run tighter than shrink wrap, and there will be no time between races to ride a lap of the course. In this case, your best option is to walk the course before you get dressed and make note of the features from your curbside perspective.

Too real for you? Then perhaps a virtual lap of the course will suffice. This is done using Google Maps Street View. I'm pretty sure that this service was developed by cycling enthusiasts specifically for bike racers who wish to take a virtual pre-ride of almost any course in the world from the comfort of their office. Frankly, I can't think of any other possible use for such a tool.

Google Maps satellite view is almost as handy. It will let you see the course, identify landmarks, and help you figure out where you're going to park on the day of the race. When used in conjunction with the measuring tool, you can measure the distance from the final corner to the finish line. And thanks to technological advances, you're not limited to measuring the course in meters. I find it helpful to know the distance in furlongs or parsecs.

You can also pick the brains of your teammates who have raced on the course earlier in the day or in previous years. They'll be able to tell you how a hill affects the pack in race conditions and which corners might give you trouble. They'll know how the sprint plays through the final turn.

Don't forget to check the wind. Knowing what the wind is doing will help you plan your attack. Remember what I said about echelons and how they can sometimes leave you out in the wind without protection. If you know a race will experience fierce winds, then you can predict when the going will get tough. Knowing the course and the direction of the wind will help you plan for those difficult sections when the wind is cutting the field to shreds (Figure 3.11).

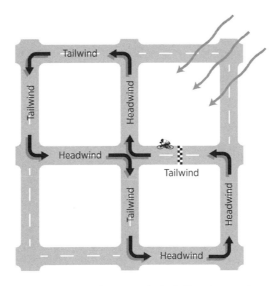

FIGURE 3.11 Criteriums often see many changes of wind direction per lap.

Chris Horner   ADVANCE INTELLIGENCE

My old teammate Rich Meeker taught me many things about bike racing, and one of them was the importance of proper intelligence gathering before the race even begins. It would be where the bike race really began. Since most riders would warm up around the course, if not directly on the course, he would talk to as many of the big players as he could find before the race, asking how their training week had been going as well as life in general. This was always followed up by a question of how their team leader was doing. Meeker used general life inquiries to gain valuable intelligence on the enemy. And he never failed to use it effectively, in our pre-race team meetings as well as during the race itself. Meeker always lived by the code "All is fair in love, war, and bike racing." ▪

GETTING PSYCHED UP (OR OUT)

Don't let the course psych you out. Don't fixate on the steepness of the hill or the odd camber of a corner. You've worked on all of your skills, haven't you? You know how to get through any corner in any weather in any sort of group. This is precisely why we work on these skills; we drove 6 hours to get here, and we don't want to drive 6 hours home without racing our bikes.

If you're racing a criterium on a course that you've never seen before, it will help to watch another race negotiate the course. Get to the race site a little early. Watch one of the other categories ride. Note where they're having trouble. Don't freak yourself out by predicting carnage; get it in your head that you're going to master the course. In fact, you're going to find a way to capitalize on the fear that is coursing through everyone else's body. You will attack through the downhill off-camber turn with the wicked crosswind right after it starts raining. And everyone will marvel at your ability to ignore the obvious perils.

I'm not suggesting that you should take undue risks in order to win a gift certificate to a local restaurant that's closed on the day of the race (ah, the coveted race prize). I'm only suggesting that you shouldn't let yourself be psyched out by a particularly hard course.

In Ann Arbor, Michigan, in the 1990s, I announced at a downtown race that had a nasty little downhill, off-camber, 60-degree right-hander. There had been a few minor crashes on it in the earlier races, so I jokingly referred to it as "the meat grinder," mainly because the pack would bunch up as it entered the corner but would emerge in single file as it came out the other end. The name stuck. It drew a line in the sand between those who could get through it well and those who let it get into their brains.

Another famous corner that I never had the pleasure of riding through (thanks to my role as an announcer) was at the bottom of "O'Hooley's Descent" at the A-to-Z Criterium in Athens, Ohio. It was a notorious hangout for the many Ohio University photojournalism majors hoping to grab a Pulitzer Prize–winning shot of a crash. The promoters erected a large wall of hay bales to protect the storefronts at the bottom of the hill. By day's end, there was hay strewn around the entire corner and a handful of happy photojournalism students.

For every race where many riders let tough corners freak them out to the point where they'll watch the last half of the race from the curb, somebody else figures out how to get through those corners and win the race. That person can be you, with preparation.

PLAYING THE ACCORDION

The accordion is a loud and wheezy musical instrument used in polka bands. I wish there were a cooler musical instrument for cycling to be associated with, but until someone comes up with a better description of how a pack moves, we're stuck with it.

The constant changes in speed during a race create a challenge all their own. The front accelerates; the pack stretches. The front slows; the pack compresses, offering riders more opportunity for running into each other. It also offers more opportunity to improve your position and launch attacks.

By knowing how the accordion effect works, you can use it to your advantage. By not understanding it, you will be frustrated.

Here's an example of frustration: slamming on the brakes every time the front riders cause the pack to slow down.

Here's an example of making it work for you: Envision yourself in a fast-moving pack that is stretched out into a long snake. Maybe it's single file, or maybe it's two or three abreast, but it's going fast. Maneuver yourself into about 12th position with a clear shot at the road ahead. The minute you sense that the front riders are slowing down, get ready. The polka is about to begin. When the front slows down, you can keep your momentum and slingshot yourself into an attack (Figure 3.12). Or you can at least be alert to others who may try the same thing. As the accordion compresses the field, many of your would-be chasers will be locked in to the pack.

FIGURE 3.12 Take advantage of the accordion effect. When the front of the pack slows down, slingshot yourself into an attack.

If you're sitting in, say, 30th position when the pace slows, you will be stuck behind the riders who fan out across the road in front of you. Or perhaps you'll be swarmed by the riders behind you. Either way, you'll be stuck in the pack without an escape route.

If you're in the back of the pack, you don't need to slam on the brakes each time the front of the field slows. That wastes energy. Instead, when the field is strung out in a long line riding at a high speed, keep an eye on the front of the pack. You'll be able to see when those riders suddenly spread out across the road, sit up, and start to coast. That's your cue to do the same. There is no need for you to hammer yourself into the back of the pack. You can immediately take your foot off the gas and ease into the bunched-up field. That's 30 extra pedal strokes that you just saved by keeping your eyes open and your head up. That adds up.

The accordion plays particularly loudly in a large field on a criterium course. A large pack going through a corner naturally gets bunched up going into the turn and strung out exiting the turn.

The accordion effect is unavoidable. Don't stress out. Just accept it as a normal movement of the peloton, and try to hold your position near the front of the pack, where the effects are less dramatic. And be thankful that each time the peloton squeezes back together, it doesn't actually sound like an accordion.

GAINING POSITION

A fellow racer once told me, "You must continuously move ahead just to stay even."

That sounds like a contradiction, but it really makes sense. Another way to say it: If you're not moving forward, you're moving backward. As speeds fluctuate and riders fight to move forward, you can find yourself shuffled to the back quite easily. Therefore, you must constantly fight to hold your position. To do that, you must stay alert. When a new wave of riders comes up from behind, you need to react immediately or get washed back 20 places.

As the finish line approaches, you must also know how to advance your position as efficiently as possible so as not to cook yourself before the final push. Yes, you can try to pass the entire pack when it's strung out in a single-file line going at supersonic speed. That's certainly one option. Not the best one, though. Better to maintain your position constantly so that you never fall back too far.

Here's more sage advice from the Mike Walden school: Never accelerate into undisturbed air. This simple truism covers a lot of ground, and it serves as a reminder to keep your nose out of the wind. It will also help you develop the ability to move up through the pack protected from the wind. This is where the elbow-bumping drill comes in handy. There will be contact between you and other riders. Get comfortable with it. Get comfortable with the verbal abuse that you'll receive as you worm your way to the front. As much as riders know that it's part of the game, they still hate it, and they'll be vocal about it.

One tip that will help you stay upright is to keep your hands on the drops. This will help prevent getting your handlebars tangled with other riders' as you thread the needle.

Keith Code, in his book on motorcycle racing called *A Twist of the Wrist*, wrote that you just need a doorway to get through. The same can be said for bike racing. You just need enough room. Riders in lower categories are less comfortable with getting too close to other riders, so they usually have a large imaginary bubble around them. Knowing this, you can squeeze between riders without much room on either side. (Refer to the "Up the alley" drill that we discussed earlier in this chapter.) The smaller you can make that invisible bubble around you, the better you'll be at moving through the pack. When someone gives you an inch, take it without hesitation.

If you consider yourself a contender for victory, you can't be shy about moving forward.

CLAUSTROPHOBIA

Not only do some riders maintain a bubble around themselves, some absolutely hate riding in the middle of the pack. It can trigger a claustrophobic response. There's nowhere to go. You have no escape. You're locked in. You have no control over your fate. Gosh, it reminds me of a past relationship.

Relax. Very seldom are you locked into a riding position in the field for very long. If you're a rider who gets a claustrophobic feeling while riding in a pack, you can simply slow down and let the field go around you. They will be more than happy to oblige. Soon you will find yourself at the back of the pack riding with others in your situation.

Of course, you can also attack. That's certainly one way to get out of the crowd, although you may only pull the other riders with you as they react to your acceleration. Then you're in an even more agitated pack, and with lower power reserves than before.

Pack claustrophobia is not uncommon. It's something that you won't find in most other sports, but you will in cycling. If you suffer from it, and if you plan to be a bike racer for any length of time, you should work on conquering the feelings. Get used to having riders on all sides of you. Develop the trust that's required to ride in the middle of the pack.

Personally, I keep one eye on what's happening immediately near me and the other eye on what's happening in the race. It's like driving on the expressway. I'm looking ahead to see what's going to affect my drive, and I'm looking around to see what's going to affect my safety.

Here's a handy mnemonic device that is taught in motorcycle safety courses: SIPDE. It stands for scan, identify, predict, decide, and execute. It's a process that happens continuously and instantaneously.

Scan the road in front of you.
Identify the items that will require your attention.

Predict what they might do.

Decide what to do about them.

Execute your decision.

And put them behind you.

If you're feeling claustrophobic, use the SIPDE process to keep track not only of the riders immediately around you but also the entire pack and the race itself.

Do whatever it takes to get over the anxiety of pack riding. Do whatever it takes to make sure you're not dangerous to other riders.

You can practice this with just one other rider. Instead of riding side by side at the normal distance of about 2 feet apart, as most cyclists do, ride side by side, overlapping elbows. It feels weird at first, but after a few thousand miles, it becomes second nature.

You can experiment with this, too: Try riding with your brake levers almost brushing the thigh of your riding partner. Or try riding with your front wheel nearly touching his or her pedal.

You will find yourself riding this close to other riders during a race. You can't let it scare you to the back of the pack.

AVOIDING CRASHES

"Riders down!"

That's the second thing that's said immediately after a crash. I can't print the first thing that's said.

Bike race crashes are a freaky thing. You never know how severe, harmless, or just plain weird the next one will be. Luckily, they're often predictable and avoidable. Note that I said "often" and not "always."

The most common causes of bike crashes are overlapped wheels and tangled or bumped handlebars. Other common causes include running into each other, losing contact with the road, and scraping a pedal. There are plenty of other ways to crash, but those top the hit parade.

First, a cyclingism that every rider must abide by is "Always protect your front wheel" (Figure 3.13). It's your stabilizing gyro, but it can also be your Achilles' heel. If anything happens to it, your day will immediately get complicated. And the higher your speed of travel, the more complicated it will get.

And watch out for other riders who are reckless with their front wheels (Figure 3.14). After riding in a pack for a few years, you get used to the spatial relationships between riders, and you become aware of when something is out of kilter. When a rider makes a side-to-side motion ahead of you, your radar

FIGURE 3.13 Protect your front wheel.

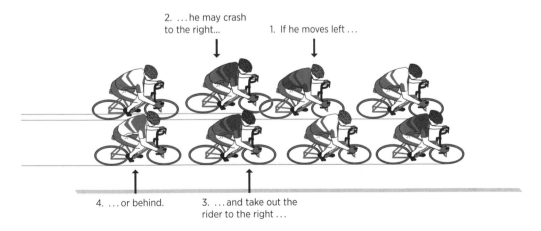

FIGURE 3.14 Watch out for other riders who are reckless with their front wheels.

should start beeping. Anyone who is overlapping that rider's rear wheel is in trouble, and since he is in front of you, you may be affected very soon. Riders who are inattentive are likely to let their front wheel be banged around.

That's not to say that you can't survive a good dose of tire rubbing. You can if you know how to handle it. Earlier I mentioned the tire-tapping drill that we conducted on the soft, grassy field. That really comes in handy when you're rubbing tires at 30 mph. It also helps you get comfortable with riding really close to the wheel in front of you.

Carrying too much speed into a turn is also bad news for a couple of reasons: centrifugal force is tough to overcome when it takes control, and a bicycle's braking system works best when the bike is moving straight ahead.

Do not panic when you hear the horrid sounds of a crash behind you. In fact, be on the lookout for a sympathy crash.

Pick the right speed before you enter the turn. Watch for other riders who are being less prudent, and remember that any crash that occurs in the corner will sweep to the outside of the turn, thanks to centrifugal force.

It's always prudent to allow a slight gap to open between your front wheel and the wheels in front of you as you enter a turn. This little cushion will allow you to react to any problems those riders encounter. If you're glued to someone else's wheel, you're at his mercy throughout the corner. If your wheel is outside his, you're relinquishing a lot of control over your line through the turn.

Do not panic when you see riders starting to fall. Push your bike forward as you apply the brakes. This distributes the braking power to both wheels and helps prevent you from going over the bars. If you have time, quickly look for an exit even if it means going off the road. If all else fails, tuck in your extremities and aim for something soft.

Do not panic when you hear the horrid sounds of a crash occurring behind you. In fact, be on the lookout for a sympathy crash. That's what happens when riders overreact to those sounds; they crash. It's a common occurrence in the lower categories, as new riders naturally tense up at the sound of danger.

It still sounds better than an accordion.

RIDING IN THE RAIN

Earlier, when I said that there would be some basics that you won't love, I was referring to this one: riding in the rain.

Not only should you get comfortable with it, you should embrace it. Come to enjoy the water in your face, the fogged-up glasses, the river running down your back, and the squishiness in your socks. Thrive on it. Revel in it.

That's not easy to do because, frankly, it's miserable. That's why very few of us amateur racers willingly train in the rain. Oh, we'll finish our ride if we get caught in it—we have to get home, after all—but very few cyclists will actually begin a training ride when it's already raining. If we're on a ride and the clouds start to get dark and ominous, we'll make a race out of it and try to beat it home. If you're a typical cyclist, you have a thrilling story about the time you outran a thunderstorm for 30 miles. (If you're a typical cyclist, you probably have a thrilling story about everything that's ever happened to you while riding.)

Pro riders have to ride rain or shine; amateurs don't. In fact, many of us use the rain as a reason not to ride. I know that there are days when I do a celebratory dance because my rain dance actually worked.

Maybe I'm exaggerating a little about the dance, but there was a real sense of relief that came with a downpour that began at 4:50 p.m., just as I was packing up and getting ready to leave the office. But then I had that now-famous conversation with my mentor who taught me to HTFU.

Since that day, some of my best results have come in the rain, and I have made an observation as to why: Most of the field either quits, crashes, or rides as if they're afraid of crashing.

If you're looking for it, you can almost detect the precise moment when someone reaches their "Oh, screw this" point. For some, it comes when that first

Chris Horner   RIDING IN THE RAIN

When it comes to riding in the rain, everyone has different views and opinions. You pack your bags and head off to the race with the belief that it will be a dry, beautiful day, and everything is going to go great. Rain starting during the stage can impact people and their motivation, but it rarely has the effect of rain before the start. When the rain comes down before the stage even starts, that is when you see who truly wants to race and who is regretting that they even bothered to pack their bags.

This was never more true than on the morning of the last stage of the Tour de 'Toona in 2000, when I was riding with the Mercury team. With Gord Fraser as our team leader, we had been fighting tooth and nail throughout the week with the Navigators team. Typically, Gord was our go-to sprinter on the team, but during this week he had been climbing so well that we had a great chance of taking the overall win.

As we headed to the start of the final stage, the downtown criterium, the rain started to fall before we had even taken our first pedal stroke for warm-up. A couple of guys on the team started moaning right away, but I turned, looked at Gord, smiled, and told him that the win was already

→

drop of rain hits the road. Others give up when they see dark clouds in the western sky. For others, it comes when they've taken too many gulps of water off the wheel in front of them. They turn off like a light switch. They sit up, stop pedaling, and retreat to the car. And that's one less person you have to worry about.

The harder it rains, the quicker the switch is thrown. If it's cold, the speed of quitting will double. If it's windy, it will triple.

RIDING IN THE RAIN, CONTINUED

in the bag. With the rain falling before the start gun even sounded, I knew two-thirds of the field was already starting to think about the trip back home.

When the gun went off, our entire Mercury team went to the front, and before we were 10 laps into it, Mike Sayers was screaming at me to slow the pace down. When I looked back, I realized that only about a third of the field was left, at best. And by the halfway point, I think there were only 20 guys left in the race. Most of the others had dropped out, I imagine, and the rest had been pulled after being ridden out of the back of the main group. The team was feeling confident because Gord had been climbing well all week, and whenever a sprinter is climbing well, you know his sprinting speed is pretty much unmatched by anyone else in the race, too. With each time bonus sprint, Gord was increasing his lead over second.

At the end of the stage, Gord had won the overall and the team had slipped Scott Moninger off the front for the stage win as a bonus. I truly believe that to be successful at any race while riding in rain, you have to be 100 percent focused and motivated! ∎

Crummy conditions will decimate the pack because, as I said before, few riders train for crummy conditions.

Riding in the rain is easier than it seems. Choose tires that give you confidence. Determine the best amount of air pressure to put in them. Learn to distribute your weight properly for the bike you're riding. Keep a soft but firm grip on the bars, like your grandfather's handshake that I mentioned earlier.

Concentrate on keeping your efforts smooth. No sudden moves. Be judicious with the brakes. Give yourself a little extra room between your front wheel and the rider in front of you. Above all, relax.

Chris Horner — MY RAIN BAG

The rain bag—a cyclist's most important yet severely underrated key to success. I learned the importance of a rain bag early in my career, when I became a European rider. Before that, I had grown up in San Diego, California, where the sun shines often, and when it does rain, let's face it, it's still 55 degrees. In Europe, though, that is never the case. If it is raining, it's usually in the 40s, if not the 30s. Ever since my early days in Europe, I have put a rain bag in every team follow car (normally there are two follow cars in each of the big races) in every race that I do. I've also learned to keep them handy when I'm not racing, with one in each of my garages and most of my cars if I am driving to any training rides.

I am known for my organization and packing skills, and that is reflected in my rain bags. For example, for 15 years, I had always packed a spare pair of cycling shoes in each rain bag, although in that time I personally had never needed them. I had loaned them out many times to riders who hadn't remembered their shoes, or broken the ones they had, but I had never needed them myself. However, I always packed them, just in case. Finally, in a very short period in 2010, I needed spare shoes on two separate occasions.

The first was during the Tour of the Basque Country: A buckle had been ripped off one of my shoes during a freak crash, and had it not been for my spare shoes, I probably would not have been able to finish the stage. I went on to win the race that year, all thanks to the spare

→

If it's any consolation, know that crashes that occur in the rain are usually less severe than those occurring on dry pavement. It's true.

Here's a little tip that I almost hesitate to give you because I want to keep

MY RAIN BAG, CONTINUED

pair of shoes. The second time I needed the shoes was in the first stage of the 2010 Critérium du Dauphiné. Again I had a buckle break because of a front wheel overlapping with my shoes, tearing the buckle off. This time my rain bag didn't save my victory, but I truly believe that it saved my RadioShack teammate Janez Brajkovic's race, and I was ready to help him as he won the race after a spectacular battle with Alberto Contador.

Now, here's what I pack inside:

- Cycling shorts
- Cycling jersey
- Cycling shoes (preferably previously worn so they are broken in and cleats are adjusted correctly)
- Undershirt
- Wind vest
- At least three different kinds of rain jacket
- At least four or five pairs of gloves for all different conditions
- Sunglasses with both clear and dark lenses
- Arm warmers
- Leg warmers
- Knee warmers
- Beanie (because I'm bald)
- Racing cap
- At least two pairs of shoe covers
- Socks

And probably a few other things thrown in for good measure. ◼

it for my own use, and I might wish to use it against you someday. If, during a bike race, the skies above you suddenly unzip and dump buckets of water on your peloton, do this: Attack. Don't think about it, just go. Take off like a bat out of hell. Everyone else will be forced to react to two things: your attack and the rain. Chaos will ensue, and you'll be in front of it all. Those riders who hate the rain will get in the way of riders who don't. You'll lose 25 percent of the field right away. You will also find out who else read this chapter.

Admittedly, a chance for that tactic comes around only once every few years, but when it works, it works well.

Unless you crash.

PEEING WHILE RIDING

Oh, yes, I'm going there. No pun intended.

Staying well hydrated is an important physiological rule that you must follow. However, excess water has to go somewhere, and during a bike race you'll need to know how to make it go somewhere else.

In the pro peloton, the riders obey the "stay hydrated" rule better than anyone. They start drinking water as soon as they wake up in the morning, and they drink coffee and espresso in the final hours before the race begins. By the time the race starts, they've already consumed enough fluids to drown a horse.

In the race, pros live by a different code than amateur racers do. They are more cooperative in spirit when it comes to voiding a bladder. As soon as the peloton rolls out of town and away from the madding crowd, 20 or 30 riders will pull over to the side of the road, stop, and water the roadside plants. They will then remount their bikes, wait for the others, form a paceline, and work together all the way back to the peloton, relieved and refreshed. A few miles later, another group operating on a different bodily schedule will collectively decide that it's time to do the same thing.

Stop giggling. It's a natural occurrence that must be tended to. In fact, it's called a "natural break." To use it in context, you could just say, "Hang on. I gotta stop for a natural."

It also happens this way in women's road races. Simply by nature of physiology, getting rid of the coffee requires getting off the bike, which in turn requires a certain cooperation among the combatants.

When a collective natural happens in a professional or a women's race, it's a heartwarming display of international sportsmanship to see 30 riders from 20 different teams stop under the banner of truce to share a moment and then form an organized chase group to regain contact with the main field.

You will never see this in American men's amateur racing, however. It just doesn't happen.

Therefore, it is important that men develop the necessary skills to urinate while in motion. You must set aside modesty and your dignified upbringing and prepare yourself for the moment in the race when your bladder takes command of your brain. What choice do you have?

You must practice this maneuver on your own. Nobody wants to see you do it. Not on purpose, anyway.

Find a slight downhill section of lightly traveled roadway. Put one foot at the bottom of the pedal stroke. Square your hips toward that same foot. Get a good grip—on the handlebars; you don't want to crash. From here, you should know how to do the rest. Your goal is to hold a straight line—with the bike. Your speed will drop naturally. You will need to take frequent breaks to resume pedaling. Good luck.

Don't worry about where "it" goes. It's going to go all over everything. Still, you have no choice; you can't ride with an overflowing bladder.

If you have a difficult time in public restrooms, then your most difficult challenge in all of this will be getting over the stage fright. It's also hard to not think of crashing while you're in this position. Just imagine the story fodder you will become for the paramedics who find you at the side of the road in a very strange position.

Once you are able to actually start the flow, however, you will be amazed at how long it lasts. Perhaps next time you won't wait so long. That's a good tip to remember.

Speaking of tips, you are not protected from indecency laws while racing or training on the public roadways of America. Keep that in mind as you practice this unique sporting move.

Once you master it, you may be anxious to show it off in front of your friends. Don't bother. It's certainly a useful skill to have, and many a race has been saved by it, but it's not a crowd-pleaser.

Just take my word for it.

All of the foregoing is easier to accomplish while wearing regular shorts, by the way. Bib shorts present a challenge. Sometimes it's easier to go out the bottom of the leg than over the waistline, depending on the height of the bib and its stretchiness. Practice this on your own on a quiet country road until you're comfortable.

Here's another obvious lesson that I've saved until the end of this section: Move to the outside of the pack when you decide to execute this maneuver in an actual bike race. I'm not sure I really needed to say this, but I can't assume that everyone has the common sense to know better.

4

HANDLING SPEED

AS A LICENSED BIKE RACER, you are responsible for controlling your bike under all conditions. Your bike handles differently at high speeds. It steers differently. It brakes differently.

But even though bike racing is all about going fast, some bike racers get spooked at high speeds. You can spot them easily; they're the ones who are getting dropped on the descents.

It's understandable, really. There is a big difference between tooling along at 20 mph, hammering at 30, and descending at 50. The road passing beneath you, the rushing air, the sounds of the chain and sprockets all work together to create an unnerving experience. High speed takes some getting used to.

Until you are a self-propelled monster able to break the sound barrier on your own, the best way to practice riding at high speed is on a descent. Find a hill. Work on your climbing technique on the way up. Work on your speed on the way down. Don't simply let the bike take you to the bottom of the hill. Weave back and forth, shift your weight from front to rear, work on your aerodynamic tuck position, and try to slow yourself down by sitting up and becoming as nonaerodynamic as you can.

You'll discover that a simple move in any direction will have a noticeable effect on your bike's handling. You'll get used to the feel of the road as it turns to a blur beneath you. And most of all, you may discover how stable the bike can be if you soften your grip and let it roll.

Know how speed affects the distribution of weight as you apply the brakes. Get comfortable with how differently the front and rear brakes perform. Learn how to feather both and how to use them to control your speed.

ECONOMY OF MOTION

If you know what to look for in a Cat. V race, you will see a great amount of wasted energy. There is wasted energy in the beginner's field because the sands of time have not worn away the extra movement that these riders are making in order to make the bike go faster. If we could find a way to harness that wasted energy, we could power a city the size of Wichita Falls.

New riders, in looking to milk greater speeds from their bike, will often recruit other muscle groups into the pedaling motion. This is most noticeable during the sprint or any time the pace is particularly high. Mainly, the wasted movement is found above the waist. The shoulders begin to rock. The arms tense. The hands hold a death grip on the bars. The teeth clench. The head wags back and forth. The hips roll. Even the ears and eyelids do anything they can to help propel the bike forward.

And none of it helps. As you evolve as a rider, though, you'll become smoother. You will soon realize that your facial muscles don't push the pedals no matter how much you try. Later you will learn that your arms aren't supposed to do much more than provide leverage and balance. The sooner you learn this, the better. In fact, you should practice it on your next ride.

Now, what happens when you watch a Pro/I/II field? You see a ballet.

Chris Horner   WHO'S FAST, WHO ISN'T

The more experienced you become as a cyclist, the easier it is to spot riders with less or even no experience. The first is the easiest to identify: The rider is simply incapable of holding his or her line from left or right and is opening up gaps behind the rider in front. You can find this on just about any group ride, and believe it or not, even at the Tour de France level. Of course, at the highest levels of bike racing, it is not so much lack of experience or lack of knowledge that you are seeing; more often, a rider's pure ability is being pushed to the limits. Or perhaps that rider has crashed recently and is now, for lack of a nicer word, just plain scared! Either way, it is important to spot these riders and avoid being anywhere near them when the speeds are high and the roads are technical.

During the 2012 Tour de France, there was one rider whose handling skills had gone so haywire from his many recent crashes during the season that every other rider in the field was racing to start the descent in front of him. Anyone behind him would get a pretty entertaining show as riders blew past him to get far, far away. Believe it or not, it was to the point that at dinner each night, everyone on the team would have a story of how bad he looked in the corner as they were passing him while trying to close the gap he had just opened up on the rider in front. Even worse, sometimes multiple stories were told by multiple riders, all on the same descent—only from different corners!

Trust me, you don't want to be that guy, so pay very close attention to this part of the book. . . . ◲

Top-level riders race with a graceful, almost poetic economy of motion that simply comes with time in the saddle. They are, for the most part, motionless above the waist. There's an old maxim in cycling that says a rider should be so smooth on the bike that someone could "build a house of cards on their back." (I don't think they really took the wind into account when they came up with that maxim.)

Elite riders develop an efficient pedal stroke, control over their breathing, and a suppleness that absorbs all the extraneous chatter of the road. The energy wasted in a Pro/I/II field, if harnessed, could provide enough power to light up the left-field scoreboard at Fenway Park.

(For those of you who aren't familiar with Fenway Park, its unlit left field scoreboard is operated by hand by people who have the coolest job in the world but the most cramped workspace.)

Obviously, bodies aren't robots. There is natural movement in the upper body during the pedal stroke, but in the experienced rider this motion is in harmony, not conflict, with what the rest of the body is doing. It's a reaction to the powerful pedaling motion of the legs, but it's only a reaction, not a cause.

So it's not a rigid requirement to be smooth, but it sure does help.

Proper form is important in cycling. It's something that can be taught, but I would advise that you choose your teacher wisely. Sometimes the best teacher is simply time.

CONSERVATION OF ENERGY

The concept of "economy of motion" is related to "conservation of energy." You must save your matches and burn them only when you really need to. Note that I didn't say that you can or should save your matches; I said you must . . . unless, of course, you have an endless supply of energy that never runs out. If so, this book is unnecessary.

You enter each race with a fixed amount of energy. Yes, you may recharge your batteries at certain points during the race, but your batteries have a finite charge. Use it wisely.

(I know it's confusing for me to use both batteries and matches as fuel metaphors. I can't help it.)

Not only must you use your energy wisely, you must also learn to turn it off when not in use and make a conscious effort to rest during those slower moments in the race. For example, if the pack is strung out in single file and the pace is so high that you're seeing cross-eyed, you'll be at full throttle. But when it's just cruising along at a normal pace, you must use only that which is necessary to maintain your position. Nothing more.

On. Off. On. Off. Don't waste angry pedal strokes that you'll need later.

Conserving energy means finding the draft and sticking to it like glue, knowing that it's your ticket to 100 percent of the speed for 70 percent of the energy.

Inexperienced riders, after drafting along in the pack at 28 mph for a while, get used to the amount of effort that it takes to ride at that speed. When the pace slows down to 24 mph, it feels a lot easier. They get fooled and become less concerned with finding the draft. They'll drift out of the draft and pedal along unaware of how much energy they're using (Figure 4.1). However, 24 mph

FIGURE 4.1 The misperception of speed: If the pack slows and the effort drops, you may drift out of the draft and burn energy needlessly.

is still a good rate of speed, which means they should be tucked in behind someone else. This misperception of speed can cause a rider to burn matches without realizing it.

Always let other people stick their noses into the wind while you hide yours. Don't worry; there will always be willing candidates. In a pack of 100 riders, there are 99 places to hide.

In no other sport is so much emphasis placed on hiding (with the obvious exception being the ICHSA, better known as the International Competitive Hide-and-Seek Association).

This is the part of the game that frustrates athletes who come to cycling from other sports. They have a hard time understanding why a roadie will sit on your wheel throughout the whole race and then sprint around you at the end.

It's OK to release a devious laugh.

That's bike racing. The race is won by the rider who spends energy at the right time, not the rider who spends the most energy.

Another way to conserve energy is to avoid dramatic changes in speed. Just as stop-and-go driving hurts gas mileage, constantly changing speeds depletes your energy. Sure, a bike race is full of fluctuations in speed, but anticipating speed changes will help you minimize this effect. For instance, if you know that the riders in front of you will have to slow down to negotiate a turn, then you should know that it's unnecessary to zoom into the turn, slam on your brakes, and sprint out of the turn.

Experienced riders have learned to avoid unnecessarily hard accelerations and hard braking. It is in their mind-set to be as energy efficient as possible with every turn of the pedals.

When you think about it, conserving energy really starts the minute you wake up on race day. (It actually starts well before then, but that falls under the heading of training, and I promised not to go down that road.) This includes limiting the amount of extra walking you do before your race and reducing the nervous energy that you expend along the way—fretting over being late, dithering about whether you packed everything, worrying about eating right, stressing out over getting a good starting position, trying not to stab yourself when you pin your number on, and so on. All of those things use energy that has to come from somewhere. The better you are at staying cool, the less energy you will burn unnecessarily. Save it for when you want to explode in a fireball of speed.

Speaking of exploding in a fireball, one of the biggest drains of nervous energy is the fear of crashing. This saps riders faster than anything else. It causes them to ride with tension in their bodies during the race. Ironically, this tension is what causes you to ride like a squirrel, which often causes crashes. Break that cycle by forcing yourself to relax from the moment you begin your race-day routine.

DESCENDING

Without question, the highest speeds in your cycling career will come on descents. Descending in a pack of riders is one of the craziest parts of the sport, and one that requires a great amount of trust. This is where you will develop your own threshold for fear, but you can't let it become a blind spot. If I know it's your blind spot, I will attack you on the descent.

To overcome your trepidation, give yourself peace of mind: Start by making sure everything on your bike is adjusted properly. A worn or maladjusted headset, worn tires, worn brake pads, a slipping shoe cleat—any of these is a disaster waiting to happen. Make sure your wheels are seated correctly in the dropouts and that the quick-release skewers are tightened properly.

(I have a friend who, upon being informed that his rear skewer had worked itself loose, reached back with his left foot and pounded it into place without slowing down. I was impressed by his footwork, but I would have felt more comfortable had he waited until I was in front of him before he did that. That

FIGURE 4.2 Sit low on the bike while descending.

is, by the way, not a skill that you need to have as a bike racer. Just stop and tighten it by hand.)

When descending at high speeds, your bike will handle better if you sit low on the bike (Figure 4.2). Do this by lowering your upper body, placing your hands on the drops, and keeping one pedal low with your weight on it.

I can easily spot someone who has done a lot of mountain biking. He'll descend a hill with his feet located at 9 o'clock and 3 o'clock and his weight evenly distributed on the pedals. He may have his butt off the saddle, too. He does this to absorb bumps on the trail when he is mountain biking, but this position makes him unstable on a road bike because it puts his weight high on the bike, not down low, where it should be.

True, there are times when road riders will descend with their feet in this position and their weight distributed evenly, but only when in an aerodynamic tuck position on a straight section of roadway. They are sacrificing bike handling for speed.

The same principles that we learned while cornering apply in the curves: Keep your weight low. Do this by keeping the outside pedal in the down position, and use the countersteering technique as you carve through a curve. Slow yourself to a safe cornering speed before you enter a curve. Look through the turn, not at the ground.

Because you're going much faster now, you must open the window of time you have to react as much as possible by looking far out in front of you. Make quick decisions about what to do about bumps, rocks, sand, other riders, corners, etc. Again, your decisions should be quick, but your actions must be smooth and graceful.

In Chapter 3, we talked about SIPDE, a technique taught in motorcycle safety courses. If ever there were a time to put it to work, it's when you're hurtling down a mountain in full tuck with no room for error.

> *If ever there were a time to put SIPDE to work, it's when you're hurtling down a mountain in full tuck with no room for error.*

For example, let's say as you *scan* the road ahead, you *identify* a rock in the apex of a curve. You *predict* that it's not going to move. You also predict that hitting it might cause your front wheel to slip out from under you. You can then predict an ambulance ride to the hospital. You *decide* to alter your course by just a smidge. You *execute* by going around it.

Disaster averted.

Another example: You scan the road ahead, and you identify a rider who is approaching a curve at a bad angle. You predict that he will have to move to his left to negotiate the turn safely. Unfortunately, that's where you happen to be riding. You must decide between allowing him room to set up for the turn or running him off the road and over a cliff. You execute by being a good guy and moving over, generously allowing him to have grandchildren someday.

All of that has to take place in milliseconds. And you must quickly move on to the next item; don't let your mind get fixated on something you just passed. Keep your attention focused on what's in front of you.

That entire thought process needs to become second nature. You can't afford to give too much attention to any one thing because many other things are requiring your attention. There's no time to think about the small rock that's sitting in the roadway at the apex of the turn. You must deal with it while you're looking for more.

You should also develop your own tuck position. There are plenty to choose from. One popular tuck seen in the Tour de France is to lean well forward, place your nose on the stem, rest your hands on the brake hoods, put your knees together, tuck your elbows into your chest, and stick your butt in the air. That one is fast and frightening. Another popular descender's position is to scoot far back in the saddle and lower the upper body as far as it will go. This is more stable and easier to change when necessary. Experiment with different positions until you find one that you're most comfortable with.

You know what I'm going to say next about descending, don't you? Practice, practice, practice. Like all of the other aspects of cycling, your descending skills need to become second nature so that you can focus on the race. If you're too concerned with negotiating the course safely, you're going to miss what's happening tactically.

There's not much to be gained by being a superfast descender, but there's plenty to be lost by being a bad one.

SELF-MADE SPEED

The speed that you get from descending is natural speed provided to you—free of charge—by gravity. You can add to it by pedaling, but all you really have to do is control the bike and accept nature's gift. Another type of speed that you must handle comfortably is the speed produced by hammering—riding flat out in the big ring in a fast-moving group. In a bike race, you will go much faster in the pack than you've ever gone on your own, and you will hold that speed for much longer periods. It's exhilarating. It's life-changing. But you must be able to handle this group-made, synergistic speed.

Again, economy of motion comes into play because the slightest push or pull on the handlebars will affect your line. And since you're in a paceline or fast-moving peloton, you must maintain your awareness of what other riders are doing.

It's hard to attain this type of speed while on a club training ride because most clubs lack sufficient horsepower to sustain it for any length of time. It's easier to find this kind of pack speed on a Tuesday-Night Worlds (TNW) ride, where more riders make the pace go higher, but the types who do those rides aren't usually welcoming of people who are learning how to go fast. They want you to already have that knowledge before you join their ride.

(We'll discuss the Tuesday-Night Worlds later. All you need to know at this point is that a TNW ride is faster than anything else known to humankind. Your parents, teachers, barber, and letter carrier don't want you to know about TNWs. They are banned on 50 continents and 17 other planets. They're also a lot of fun. Note: In some parts of the country, this ride is held on a Wednesday night. If you are looking for the Tuesday-Night Worlds in those parts of the country, check back on Wednesday.)

MOTORPACING

In lieu of a fast group that is welcoming of inexperienced riders, the best way to replicate race pace and get comfortable with racelike speed for prolonged periods is to take pace behind a motorcycle.

Disclaimer: Motorpacing is life-threateningly dangerous. It is probably unlawful where you live. It is fraught with peril. It is frowned upon by everyone. But it will also make you a faster bike racer.

If you can't find 20 other riders to maintain 30 mph for 2 hours, buy a small motorcycle, make a few safety alterations to it, and teach a close personal friend how to ride it at a steady speed.

The safety alterations that you need to make to the motorcycle are designed to protect your bicycle's front wheel and keep it from tangling with the rear of the motorcycle. This involves fashioning some sort of roller system to be mounted on the rear end of the motorcycle at the point where it would contact your bike's wheel. The rollers should spin when the wheel bumps into them, thus preventing your wheel from coming to a dead stop.

You will ride in the draft of that motorcycle at speeds that you could never generate on your own. Basically, motorpacing is a dream come true for wheel-suckers everywhere: The motorcycle is your new training partner that never tires and never asks you to take another pull.

Before you find a quiet road on which to train, I strongly insist that you have a cyclist as the motorcycle rider, not just a friend who knows how to ride a motorcycle. There's a lot of nuance in doing this activity safely, and a cyclist will understand those nuances more readily. I also insist that this cyclist be a trained motorcyclist with the appropriate motorcycle endorsement on his or her license. Do not—I repeat, do not—shortcut this process. I'm also a fan of the Motorcycle Safety Foundation safety course, and I highly recommend that you both take the course before doing any motorpacing. Motorpacing is cool, but only if both you and the moto pilot are smart about it.

A motorcycle draft is bigger and stronger than anything you'll find in a bike race.

A good motorpacing workout is between 45 and 90 minutes long. It has prolonged fast periods followed by medium periods interspersed with slow periods interrupted by surprise accelerations. In other words, it's just like a race. But the long, steady, fast periods are the primary reason that you want to motorpace. You're trying to develop fast leg speed, sure, but you're also training your mind and body to handle the greater speed.

The draft behind a motorcycle is bigger and stronger than anything you'll find in a bicycle race because the driver is sitting in a position that a bike rider would never hold at 30 mph: upright. The sweet spot is huge. That's the point. That's what makes it possible to attain and hold a greater speed.

Once you get comfortable behind the moto, attack it. Take the lead on your own. See how long you last out in the wind. And when you start to fade, try to jump back into the draft when the moto catches and passes you at a steady 30 mph. If you do manage to get back in the draft, you can practice the forced recovery technique I told you about earlier. When you've fully recovered, attack again.

Isn't this fun? It most certainly is because the motorcycle never complains.

Here's another warning: Once you get used to pacing behind a moto at 30 mph for an hour, you may find yourself becoming bored by the 24 mph average speed in your next race. Take a book to read. You'll be fine.

I have a few more caveats regarding this dangerous activity.

You need to communicate clearly with your moto driver before each session. Be clear about what your workout goals are. Don't make assumptions.

The driver should make no sudden moves. The moto is replicating a pack of riders, so it should move as a pack of riders would.

I'm also a fan of having just one person at a time ride behind the moto. I've seen long lines of riders taking pace off a single moto. (This is common on a velodrome.) It can be done on the road, but I prefer to have fewer moving parts. It's easier to concentrate on the speed when you're not worried about what everyone else is doing.

Finally, you may be tempted to draft behind a car instead of a motorcycle. This is a bad idea. You can't see the road ahead. You can't spot debris in the roadway. You can't swerve around the car in an evasive action. You don't derive the same benefits behind a car; the draft is too big and too easy to find. Don't do it.

When I'm old and gray, some of my best memories of cycling will be of the time I spent motorpacing. If you are attracted to the sport by the need for speed, you will probably enjoy motorpacing as much as racing itself.

I've discussed downhill speed and the prolonged speed of motorpace workouts. I should also mention interval speed while I'm at it.

INTERVALS

While motorpacing and descending help you reach high speeds, there's nothing quite as rewarding as reaching top speeds on your own. There are plenty of predesigned training workouts for attaining your highest speed and deriving the best physiological benefit. Again, training falls outside my realm. I'm more interested in making sure you know the bike-handling skills that go with the speeds you'll reach.

One common mistake a rider can make while riding at a high speed is to look down. It's almost the natural tendency to put your head down when you're putting in a hard effort on the bike. If you're alone on a quiet stretch of road, you may get away with it. If there are other riders around you, you may not.

Djamolidine Abdoujaparov, the Tashkent Terror, won many races and wore the sprinter's jersey in all three Grand Tours, but his most infamous moment came on the Champs-Elysées in 1991 when he made his move out of the pack up the right side of the road. He had a clear view of the finish line, and he certainly had the legs to get there, so he put his head down and gave it everyth — you know where this is going, don't you?

With his head down, he had a great view of his bike and his feet but an exceedingly poor view of what lay ahead. Had he looked up, he would have seen the barricades that lined the course. He hit a barrier at 30-plus mph and tumbled into history as one of the most horrific bike crash survivors ever.

A more common result of looking down is to run into the rear wheel of the rider in front of you. You already know what that leads to.

The bad habit of looking down while riding comes from, I believe, riding on an indoor trainer in the winter months. It's very easy to fall into the posture of looking down when you're riding in your living room.

Don't do it. There is no value in looking at your feet when you're hammering forward.

Even without hitting anything, the end of a sprint (or speed interval) can be a sketchy time on the bike. As a bike race announcer, I've witnessed some frightening crashes that have taken place while (and, unfortunately, after) sprinters are crossing the finish line. There's a brief moment when riders transition from an out-of-the-saddle sprint to getting back on the saddle and coasting. That's where their line starts to wobble. Learn to hold a straight line through this period, and watch for others who don't.

Practice this when you do your interval training. Just as you practice accelerating, you must also practice decelerating. Someday you'll win a sprint for a major victory, and your friend will be shooting video of the event. If you stay

If you crash, that video will get a trillion views, all of which will be by people who want to see the winner crash.

upright, that video will get 73 views on YouTube, all of which will be by you and your family members. If you crash, that video will get a trillion views, all of which will be by people who want to see the winner crash.

Speeds ridden during a time trial are also something to get accustomed to. Time trial bikes are fun to ride because they're fast, but they're dangerous for the same reason. A lot is happening when you're riding one. The aero riding position, though sleek, isn't the most stable thing in the world. The geometry of a dedicated time trial bike is vastly different from that of a regular road bike. Transitioning from the upright riding position to the aero position (and vice versa) requires you to let go with one hand while changing your weight distribution. Braking also requires you to change your hand position.

We sacrificed a lot of handling ability when we adopted the aero riding position. Even non-TT-specialist pro riders will admit that they feel uncomfortable on their custom-fitted time trial bikes. They generally need a refresher course each time they ride in an event where the TT bike is used. The layer of dust on the top tube is usually an indication of how long it's been since their last aero ride.

You can wipe the dust off, but you can't wipe riding skills on. You must practice.

During a time trial, in an effort to gain an aerodynamic edge, riders tend to drop their heads and look down. You can get away with this for a few seconds at a time if you need to unkink your neck, but the majority of your time on a bike should be spent looking ahead, no matter how boring the scenery. (This is especially true if you are wearing a time trial helmet, as it is aerodynamic only when it is facing forward.)

Crashing in a time trial is embarrassing because everyone who sees it happen says the same thing: "Ohhhhh, man. He wasn't looking where he was going."

Next stop: YouTube.

5

ATTACKING

IT'S TIME TO TAKE EVERYTHING WE KNOW about motivation, ability, bike-handling skill, drafting, and peeing and apply it to a race.

The main objective in racing is for someone on our team to win, so in this section we will explore the many ways to get the job done. As I go through these lessons, I will move you around a lot. Sometimes you'll be in the breakaway. Sometimes you'll be the blocker. Sometimes both. Other times you will be an entire team. It may be confusing, but that's bike racing.

CREATING A BREAKAWAY

Now that we're comfortable riding in the peloton, we can focus our efforts on getting out of it. Of course, the easiest way to do that is to stop pedaling and go out the back, but since we're looking for a way to stand on the podium and not on the curb, we must go out the front door.

The breakaway is the core of bike racing tactics. It's how we improve our odds of winning the race. Being in the breakaway in cycling is like being a runner on second in baseball—you're in scoring position. Without the breakaway, we would just ride to the finish and sprint for the win, and bike racing would get old really fast. Instead, the breakaway offers a zillion (roughly) possible scenarios for each race. To break away, we must literally break free from the pack, establish a gap, and hold the gap to the finish. We must work in a cooperative effort if we're a group, or we need to settle into our time trialing rhythm if we're alone.

The initial attack can come at any time. It begins with one rider sprinting away from the rest. What happens next will determine whether the attack will start a breakaway or if it will just cause the pack to go faster. If no one reacts to it, it will become a solo breakaway. If the rider's intention was to go on a solo breakaway, he'll stick with it. If his intention was to get the party started, he'll wait for others to join him. If no one comes up to join him, he'll likely return to the protection of the peloton and try again later.

But how do you know when to attack?

You make an educated guess based on as many facts as you can gather.

First of all, consider your strengths. Are you someone who can work in a small group for a long time and still have enough energy to sprint at the end? Or are you someone who needs the protection of a larger group in order to save your energy for the end? If the former, you can go almost anytime. If the latter, you need to wait until late in the race to make your move. Or perhaps you're a lone wolf who is strong enough to hold off a thundering herd single-handedly. You can always try that.

What does the course look like? Is it flat? Hilly? Technical? Straightforward? Which of these types of courses favor your abilities? It would be suicidal for you to attack on a hilly course if you are America's worst climber. If you have mad cornering skills and the course is tight and technical, then you might be wise to have a go.

What's happening in the race? Has the pack been tooling along at 18 mph for the past few miles? If so, everyone is rested and probably waiting for something to happen. Your chances of creating a gap will be pretty slim. Is the pack strung out in a single-file line and holding a torrid pace? If so, you're not going anywhere. Instead, you have to pick a time somewhere in between.

Where are you in the pack? Are you sitting at the back? If so, you're not in a good position to do anything but watch. You're a spectator on wheels. Are you in the middle of the group? If so, you're going to burn most of your matches just to get to the front; creating a gap off the front at this point will require a super-human effort. Are you riding right on the tip of the spear? If so, you're not going to surprise anyone with your bold move. Instead, you need to be near the front with a clear path to the road ahead.

Are you attacking with a tailwind or on a descent? Those are two very easy conditions for everyone to chase you down. Are you attacking into a head-wind? That may work, but it won't be easy.

The timing of your attack is up to you, but the reality is that someone else will probably beat you to the punch anyway. Your best-laid plans of attacking at a certain point in the race are often trumped by riders who had an earlier schedule and didn't wait around for you to pull the trigger. In other words, someone is going to attack. You're as good a candidate as anyone, but the timing is the key.

Slingshot

If conditions are right for you to attack, then all you have to do is pick your moment and start mashing the pedals. You can jump with every sinew of your being and see if you can get something started, be it solo or a party.

But let's think about this for a moment. We already know that the act of accelerating and hammering will burn matches, and we know that a lone rider must fight the wind. If you are neither very strong nor very lucky, your solo attack is unlikely to succeed.

Better to find a more efficient way to launch your attack. One of the best is a two-rider slingshot, where you lead a teammate to the front, fast, and send him up the road.

Here's how it works: You are going to ride behind me in the pack in about 20th position. When your moment arrives, you will tell me to start rolling. You

Teammate   You   You die   Teammate lives

FIGURE 5.1 The two-rider slingshot attack

can use whatever command you wish. You can say, "Yep." You can say, "Go." You can cough loudly like Chevy Chase in the movie *Spies Like Us*. Just make sure I hear you.

Upon hearing this, I will accelerate with you glued to my rear wheel (Figure 5.1). When the two of us get to the front of the pack, you will already be traveling at the speed of light without ever having felt a headwind. When I pull aside, you will launch yourself into space. And, as an added bonus, I will find myself at the front of the field in the perfect position to begin the blocking procedure that will ensure your success.

You're welcome.

Many times, as a racer and as an announcer, I have seen riders launch a fierce attack from 20th position on their own. By the time they have reached the front of the pack, they've lost a lot of steam. But imagine what 20 bike lengths looks like if you don't turn on that energy until you get to the front of the field. That's a decent gap.

I'll remind you of this slingshot thing when we discuss bridging gaps, chasing breakaways, and sprinting later in this book. It's a tactic that you need to practice with your teammates a few times to make sure you're in sync with your accelerations and timing.

And you must somehow find a way to communicate your intentions to your teammate. Try to do it in a way that won't give away your escape.

Broadcasting Intentions

Having just told you the importance of getting up to speed and making a clean break, I need to tell you a contradictory tactic.

Sometimes a rider will attack at a speed that is slow enough for others to jump on board but also fast enough to discourage everyone from joining the party (Figure 5.2).

These attacks are usually launched by dominant riders who can create enough speed to ride away from the field with relative ease but who don't want

Step 1: First rider goes.

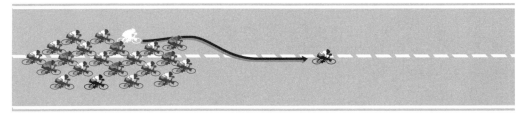

Step 2: Second rider joins.

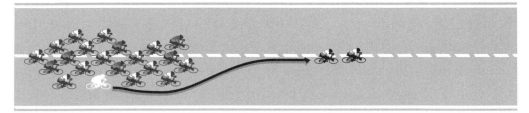

Step 3: Breakaway riders immediately rotate to extend lead.

FIGURE 5.2 The broadcast break

to go solo. They know that the breakaway will succeed as long as they approve of who comes along for the ride. And that's what they're doing: broadcasting their intentions. They're saying, "OK, kids, I'm attacking now; who's coming with me? Join me if you dare. If I like you, I'll let you stay."

They may look over their shoulders while they're attacking to see if anyone is coming with them. They may look under their arms. They won't explode out of the pack, but they will move with purpose. Only the serious are welcome to join. Once they successfully establish a gap, they will then decide whether they like the makeup of the group. If they don't like it, they'll sit up and refuse to cooperate. If they like it, good-bye.

(Imagine, for a moment, having the kind of strength it takes to create a breakaway and then having the wherewithal to decide if you even want it to continue. Most of us get into a breakaway situation and work desperately to make it stick, thus cooking ourselves in the process. The idea that we may not want it to succeed is a foreign concept. Well, that's pro bike racing, and it happens at the higher levels of amateur riding, too.)

By not exploding into an attack to initiate a breakaway, riders with roll-off-the-front power won't burn too many matches. It's easier to recover from a measured acceleration, so they'll be ready to go again soon if it fails, whereas an explosive attack off the front may require a rider to spend time recovering in the pack. During those recovery periods, the rider is vulnerable to attacks from other riders and may be unable to respond when they come.

Timing is everything with a broadcasted breakaway. Riders who use this maneuver will usually pick a time when the pack is still recovering from a previous hammer session. In those moments when we are all catching our breath, the dominant rider will strike at our throats by rolling off the front, taking the strong with him.

It's OK to hate them.

Faux Attack

Would you ever attack without intending to follow through?

Sure.

Sometimes a rider just wants to see who's awake and alert. It's fun to attack, if only to see who will respond. In the early stages of a race, you will have no trouble stirring up some sort of action, whether you are serious about it or not, because everyone is fresh and willing. Later in the race, you can use this tactic to find out who still has gas in the tank.

Another reason to make an uncommitted attack is to wear down the competition. By making them respond, you're making them expend energy. You're essentially softening them up for a more serious attack that will come from your teammate later in the race.

Fake attacks come in rapid succession, one after the next. Each time the same team will be the instigator, and each time it will take just a little more zip out of the legs of others. It can be an effective tactic if you have enough strong riders on your team to keep the peloton under stress.

Another version of the fake attack is to attack up one side of the road, taking the entire pack with you, only to be counterattacked by your own teammate up the other side of the road.

It's all part of a plan. Picture this: The wind is hitting your peloton from the right. You attack up the left side of the road, and you string out the field in the left gutter. Suddenly, up the right side of the road your teammate attacks on his own. Now, in order for riders to catch your teammate, they must bridge across the width of the road and into the wind. He has an immediate gap. That may be all it takes to discourage anyone from following. Or at least it will discourage the riders who are on the bubble.

That's another thing to consider. As I said at the beginning, not all riders have the same capabilities and strengths. If an attack goes off the front, the riders nearest to it may not be willing or physically able to respond. If Rider X attacks and the first five riders on the front of the field (let's call them Rider 1, Rider 2, Rider 3, Rider 4, and Bachelor 5) are cooked from a previous effort, then Rider 6 is already five bike lengths behind before he begins to respond. That's a gap. If Rider X's intention is a solo breakaway, he's away, and the chase is on.

Rider 6 will likely hesitate because he's expecting R1, R2, R3, R4, and B5 to react. If they don't, Rider X has a bigger lead.

That's a smart attack. Rider X assessed the strength of the riders around him, and he attacked when those riders had been weakened in battle.

I hate Rider X. Unless he's on my team.

Bungee Attack

We've all seen them. We've all made comments about them. We are powerless to stop them. The ill-fated bungee attack is a phenomenon that we see most frequently in the lower, less experienced categories. Riders will attack with all the heart and hubris of Hercules, but they will only last for about a mile. It's as if they're attached to an invisible bungee cord. They come back as fast as they go out.

In almost every racing community, there is at least one local racer who is known for his bungee attacks. This rider, however, is completely unaware that he is doing it. He truly has every intention of breaking away. However, as the old saying goes, "The spirit is willing, but the flesh is weak."

I'm reminded of an episode of the TV show *M*A*S*H* in which there was a character named "5 O'clock Charlie" who flew over the encampment every day at precisely 5 p.m., dropping a bomb far off target, to the hearty guffaws of the 4077th staff.

That is the bungee attack. With almost clocklike precision, the attack comes at a meaningless point in a race, lasts for about a mile, gets reeled in without any real effort, and gets unceremoniously spit out the back, to the hearty guffaws of the 4077th staff.

The thing is, one of these days, it just might work.

Size of the Break

If you were unpopular in high school (perhaps due to the fact that you were riding your bike a lot), you will enjoy the instant popularity you get when you attack in a bike race. You will be the talk of the peloton.

Your attack is called a "flyer" for the first few moments. The flyer is bike racing's way of running something up the flagpole to see if anyone salutes. If no one responds to your attack, then you officially become a solo breakaway. If that was your intention, go for it. Your flyer will then become a solo breakaway starring you and you alone. If, however, your intention was to start a break-away group, you need to establish a decent gap, hold a steady tempo, and wait to see if anyone comes across the gap to join you. If no one joins you, you can slow down and allow the field to catch up.

(If no one joins you, don't take it personally. Though it feels like you sent out party invitations and no one showed up, I can assure you that's not what's happening. They just had other plans. At least that's what I tell myself.)

Perhaps one or two riders will join. If so, you've achieved your mission. Party on! Get the rotating paceline working immediately, and hope for the best.

If three or four riders come across the gap, that's OK. In fact, seven riders is a decent breakaway size. But if 20 riders come across the gap to join you, your party is probably too big. The neighbors will complain. The police will come. They'll shut you down.

There's no formula for success in regards to the size of a breakaway. I've seen breakaways of all different sizes. It can be one rider, two riders, or 20 riders. Generally, though, the larger the breakaway, the smaller its chances of success. A breakaway consisting of just one rider is monumental. A two-rider breakaway is really hard but happens all the time. A three-rider breakaway is certainly doable. But in my opinion, the ideal number of riders in a break-away is between four and eight. That's large enough to have horsepower while allowing the breakaway riders time to recover in the rotation. It's also small enough to be nimble through the corners. That's where you'll gain time on the thundering herd behind you.

A breakaway group larger than eight has too many moving parts to be effi-cient. It'll accordion in the turns, and gaps will inevitably form. Pretty soon the break will be expending more energy trying to keep itself together than sepa-rating itself from the pack.

Once your breakaway forms, you must quickly assess whether or not it's going to work based on the way it moves. If it lumbers, it'll die a quick death.

Once you've determined that your breakaway group is working well together, you can turn your attention to its actual composition. Who is in it? In terms of a rolling poker game, what type of hand have you been dealt? Did you draw the ace, king, and queen of hearts in this breakaway? Or were you dealt the two of diamonds, the three of clubs, and a joker?

In most parts of the country, everyone knows everyone else. They know which riders are aces and which are not. They know very quickly whether they have the right combination for success.

And what about the number of teammates? Does our team have more than one rider in the breakaway? The dynamics will change if it does.

Ideally, our team should strive to have 20 to 30 percent of the riders in the breakaway. So in a breakaway of eight, our team should have at least two riders in it. With more riders in the breakaway, we will have more options. We'll need those options as we get closer to the finish line.

Granted, it's often impossible to get just one rider into a breakaway, let alone two. Still, that's the guideline you should follow to improve your chances of winning. Think of it this way: If you have 8 teammates in a pack of 80 riders, your team makes up 10 percent of the field. So if you have 1 rider in a 10-rider breakaway, you've only preserved the odds. The idea of a breakaway is to increase your odds. The only way to do that is to add teammates to the breakaway.

Working with a Teammate

If you find yourself in a successful breakaway group that also includes one of your teammates, you have an advantage that you need to need to capitalize on. Quickly decide which of you has a better chance in the sprint. That rider should work less in the breakaway while the other works to keep the breakaway going. You need to sort this out quickly and figure out how to win the race. It gets embarrassing after a race when you hear people say, "Gee, they had two guys in a six-man breakaway. Why didn't they win it?"

You must communicate with your teammate and decide on a course of action before you get too close to the finish. Or perhaps you already practiced this during a training ride.

We'll talk about ways to win from a breakaway later.

BREAKAWAYS THAT DON'T WORK

If you're in a breakaway that just can't seem to work efficiently, it may be due to a few different reasons.

1. Chemistry, or lack thereof.
2. Someone may not want it to succeed. Look around to see if anyone is messing up the rhythm. Perhaps it's Miss Ohio, who has been given explicit orders by her team captain to not cooperate with the breakaway. She may be in the breakaway only to keep tabs on it, or she may have something else in mind.

At a circuit race in Kalamazoo long ago, I managed to get into a six-man breakaway, but it wasn't working very well together. I noticed that one rider was sitting on the back refusing to work while the other five riders worked really hard trying to make the breakaway succeed.

A few laps later, the unwilling rider went straight to the front of the small group as if he had been shot from a World War II cannon (presumably from a local cemetery) and started driving the pace up. We had been joined by one of his teammates, so suddenly he was motivated to make this breakaway stick.

In fact, he had received information from a coach standing along the course that a teammate was in the process of bridging across the gap all alone. That was why he had refused to cooperate. He was waiting for his teammate to catch up. Once he did, the breakaway started to work really well.

3. Although we think that everything has to do with tactics and teamwork, a more likely explanation for a failing breakaway may be that riders simply don't know how to run a smooth paceline. That's why I suggested that you should feel free to give instructions or encouragement. Never assume that everyone has the same amount of experience. Don't assume that everyone has read this book. And if someone else takes the directorial lead in the breakaway, never assume that they're the most experienced rider in the group. They're only proving to be the most verbal at this point.

So, to be clear, the basic plan is to get a breakaway started and make sure that it has enough of our teammates in it to give us a better chance at winning the race. And while our team is represented in the breakaway, we still have work to do in the main pack. Lots of work.

Blocking

In the movies, when criminals flee the scene, they run really fast, hoping to put distance between themselves and their pursuers. To slow the progress of their would-be captors, they usually throw garbage cans into the path of whoever is chasing them. The chaser trips over the garbage can, sending lettuce and banana peels everywhere.

In bike racing, we use teammates in place of garbage cans.

(If you've ever seen my teammates at the dinner table, you would know that this analogy isn't far off the mark.)

Once the gap is established, the rest of our team should go to the front of the field and work to disrupt any chase efforts.

As I mentioned earlier, in the olden days of toe clips and wool jerseys, blocking was done in a very direct manner. If I wanted to impede your chasing effort, I would literally go the front and slow down in front of you, forcing you to do the same. To have a more pronounced effect, I would do this in the corners, where you would have less room to pass me. As we came out of the turn, I would drift to the outside apex and slow down, forcing you into the curb. You would have to use your brakes to avoid crashing. This would steal your momentum and pad the breakaway's lead by a few seconds at each turn.

The same tactic was used on the open road. Six or seven riders from a single team would line up across the front of the peloton and block the entire width of the road to prevent anyone from moving forward. The pack would crawl along at 15 mph while the breakaway rode off into the sunset with all of the prize money.

We don't use that tactic very often today. Today we endeavor to disrupt the rhythm of the rotation at the front of the pack simply by refusing to pull through when our turn comes—not just once but several times. As we learned in our earlier lessons on paceline rotation, rhythm and consistency are key components in maintaining speed. Without that rhythm, the pace never gets going. And it takes only one rider to mess up the synergy. Here they do it on purpose.

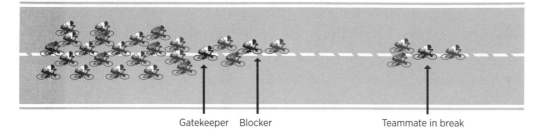

Gatekeeper   Blocker   Teammate in break

FIGURE 5.3 Blocking from the front

As a blocker, this requires a constant effort to hold your spot at the front of the field and continue to be an annoyance to everyone around you (Figure 5.3). Be prepared to take a load of verbal abuse from other riders, who will call you names and speak ill of your family. This is part of the game. They will try to goad you into cooperating while they are secretly admiring your devotion and loyalty to your team. At least, that's what you should tell yourself when they pummel you with insults and threats.

In many respects, it is more difficult to be a blocker than to be a breakaway rider. In the breakaway, you're focused solely on maintaining a fast, steady speed. As a blocker, you must constantly fight to maintain your position. Your head must be on a swivel looking for anyone who might try to attack. You will change your speed a million times, which will tire you out. And after the race, you will get nothing.

That's bike racing.

Another way to block is to go fast. Pretty fast, anyway. I know it sounds crazy, but it's a popular tactic that you need to know.

Picture this: We're in a race. There is a breakaway off the front, and our team isn't represented in it. (What were you doing? Taking a nap? Shame on you.) We know that it's now our job to go to the front and pick up the pace, but someone else is already doing it. It's the teammate of one of the riders in the breakaway. He appears to be breaking a cardinal rule of bike racing: Never chase your own teammate.

Chris Horner   DECEIVING THE FIELD

I used this tactic to perfection once, many, many years back. During what was maybe my second or third year as a professional, a good friend of mine, Derek, informed me as we stood on the start line that this would be his last race. We were doing a Pro/I race in the Los Angeles area at the time. Derek and I trained together whenever I was in the Visalia area, and of course we had chatted throughout the many years whenever we would see each other at races.

With about 10 laps to go, Derek took a solo flyer off the front. I immediately went to the front of the pack and started to put in an effort that looked like I was trying to chase him down. But in reality, for the next five laps, I was actually slowing the pace of the field, riding at least a few miles an hour slower than the speed he was doing off the front. It took until about five laps to go for everyone to realize that the time gap was going up and not down, at which point the other teams finally started to race. But by then, it was too late. Derek had at least a 1:30 gap with only five short laps to go and easily took the win at the end.

I still see him around once in a while, some 15 years later, and always remind him of how I helped him win the last pro-am race of his career. Now he's my go-to electrician, and his son is old enough to make use of all my old gear as he gets going in a junior racing career of his own. ◼

As he continues to hold a steady speed of 24 mph, we fall into a false sense of security. We assume that because he's riding this fast, he's surely gaining on the breakaway.

He is not. In fact, he is losing ground steadily because the breakaway is traveling at 26 mph. We are losing time.

This is an effective ploy because it capitalizes on a roadie's natural tendency to let others do the work. All a rider has to do is go to the front of the pack and hold a tempo that can be construed as brisk, and everyone will fall in behind him like ducklings. Strange but true. And we have to fight to overcome that natural tendency by passing the lead rider and pushing the pace on our own. No one is going to do it for us. We missed the break. The onus is on us.

Gatekeepers

The key to a breakaway actually becoming a breakaway is establishing, maintaining, and preserving the gap. The larger the gap, the more it deters others from closing it or crossing it. The smaller the gap, the easier it is to close or cross; therefore, everyone and his brother will try.

Once the breakaway has a gap, our job as "blocker" also becomes that of "gatekeeper," controlling the quality of the riders who go across the gap to join the breakaway. Even in the early moments, we have to decide which riders to let go and which ones to corral.

Who gets permission to pass our blocking tactics? Well, we're only going to let riders pass who can help the breakaway succeed but not beat our teammate. Every time a rider attacks in an attempt to go across the gap, we need to have a pair of eyeballs on him and make the determination. We're the bouncer who stands outside the club and decides whom to allow into the party.

That's a lot to think about, and you must make these decisions while you're rolling along at 50 mph. (I round up. Slightly.)

Chasing, Bridging, Reeling, Catching

The difference between chasing and bridging is a matter of semantics and context.

I'm chasing when I'm bridging, but I may not be bridging when I'm chasing.

Let's imagine that the breakaway has a 20-second lead. If I want to join it alone, I need to attack, make a clean break, and catch the leaders without towing anyone across the gap with me. In essence, I need to bridge the gap. If I made that sound easy, then I left out some key words: *difficult, annoying, wheelsuckers.*

While I'm in the gap, I'm chasing. And since my intention is to catch the breakaway, then I'm also bridging.

"Chasing" can also be used in the context of reeling in the breakaway. Chasing it down. Bringing it back. In this case, I have no interest in joining the party. My intention is to bring it all back together and squash their dreams. Therefore, I don't care if I have wheelsuckers coming with me. I'm not bridging; I'm reeling in the break like a sea bass.

Chasing and reeling require a concerted and persistent effort to overcome the effects of blocking by other teams. This is as close as cycling can get to having a line of scrimmage; some teams are trying to gain yardage while others are trying to stop them. It makes for intense action at the front of the peloton. This means that those who have a vested interest in catching the breakaway must contribute to the workload at the front of the field. Wishes and dreams won't bring the breakaway back; only hard work will.

(Unfortunately, that blocking action doesn't translate to television very well. If it did, we'd see a lot more bike racing on TV.)

As I mentioned, most of it has to do with semantics. At no point in a race do you have to declare what you're doing, but it comes in handy to know the terminology when your teammate turns to you and tells you to bridge across, chase down, or reel in the breakaway. You'll want to know what he's talking about.

Bridging Distance

Smart riders who wish to join a breakaway know that it's foolish to chase too soon. If you chase when the gap is relatively small, everyone will want to go with you. Conversely, if you wait too long, the gap may be too big, and you'll

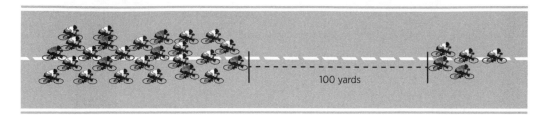

100 yards

FIGURE 5.4 Bridging distance. Warning: 100 yards at 30 mph is much more than 100 yards.

fade halfway across. When you do, you will effectively cut the distance in half for those riders behind you. Essentially, you become a stepping stone for them. They can jump across to your draft, catch their breath, and then jump across the rest of the gap.

You need to know your own optimal distance for this (Figure 5.4). How far can you let the gap grow before you can jump across it in one fast, hard effort? And how quickly can you can get across the gap, recover from that effort, and begin to contribute to the synergy of the breakaway? You don't want to cook yourself going across the gap and then blow up when you reach the break.

When a breakaway forms, be patient and wait in the field until the gap grows a little. Let the leash out, so to speak. Wait until the gap is nearly uncrossable. The longer that distance, the more it will deter others from trying it. Of course, it will depend on the course profile, the weather, and how much time you spent standing around the water cooler at the office all week. When the distance is right, make your move. Get across the gap in one hard effort. Try not to get bogged down in the middle of no-man's-land. It's a slow death if you do.

It's fun to watch a rider tackle a long bridge successfully. It's one of the hardest things to do in a bike race, and it's worthy of admiration. You know that there are doubters in the field who will be certain the gap is too large. If you're the guy doing the bridging, that's exactly what you want them to think.

This is something that you can practice on weeknights with your team-mates. Divide the group into two smaller groups with a 20-second gap between them, and conduct interval drills bridging from the trailing group to the leading group. Doing intervals in this manner will teach you the mental aspect of chasing and will also help build the strength and endurance you need to make the move succeed in a race.

Chris Horner   BRIDGING THE GAP

It was 2004, and I was riding on one of the smallest professional teams in the United States—if not the world—Webcor Builders. Webcor is a commercial building contractor and a longtime supporter of cycling, and the team they put together was mostly made up of guys with full-time construction jobs. Before the start of the season, I thought we might be able to win a few stages here or there during the year but wasn't expecting miracles with a team full of "working stiffs," along with the established pro Charles Dionne and me. Our first stage race together was the San Dimas Stage Race, in southern California, and to my surprise, it would prove to be the start of an amazing year.

I had won the opening uphill time trial in San Dimas, and we were now starting the second stage, which featured a hilly circuit race. Halfway through the stage, a fairly large break got away and gained some significant time, but the Webcor guys were doing a great job of limiting the damage. About 3 miles before the start of the final lap, the gap was down to about 1:20.

We were coming up on the masters field, which was getting ready to finish. The official driving the lead motorcycle for our field let the break

→

BRIDGING THE GAP, CONTINUED

pass the masters but held up our field to allow the masters to finish. I was arguing vehemently with the official driving the motorcycle to let us pass, but he refused, telling me that since there was no way that we would ever catch the break with only one lap to go, the delay was not going to change the outcome of the race.

When the official told me that, I gave him one of my "You're crazy" looks and immediately headed back to my teammates to get organized. I told the team that as soon as we crossed the start/finish line, the four remaining guys needed to go 100 percent for the next 3 miles, bringing us to the bottom of the first climb on the circuit as fast as they possibly could go. Each one rode all out until they blew, going so hard that it looked like we were coming into the final sprint as we entered the base of the first climb.

As we came out of the final corner before the climb, I told my final remaining teammate, Justin England, to start sprinting with everything he had. As soon as he blew, I took off. By the time we hit the second and final hard climb on the circuit, I had caught the break. I followed the final attack out of the break that made it to the line to sprint for the win. Not only did I get the win, but I also received an apology from the motorcycle official. ◾

CHASING YOUR OWN TEAM

Here's a good question: Would we ever need to reel in the breakaway when our team is represented in it? Yes, plenty of times. Although it is a basic racing rule to never chase down your teammate, it's a rule that is broken all the time when the situation calls for it.

If our team is greatly outnumbered or outgunned in the breakaway, we would be wise to reel it in and start over. Last place in the breakaway is just one spot better than first place in the field sprint. We can do better than that. If we have the weakest rider in a four-man breakaway, we have to decide if our team will be happy with fourth place. If so, we'll let him stay there and enjoy the ride. If not, then we need to make a change.

Or perhaps our teammate in the breakaway suddenly realizes that he's in trouble. He's sitting at the tail end of the breakaway, waving frantically, trying to get our attention. That can't be good. He's bonking, cramping, or maybe he just remembered that he was supposed to pick up his son at soccer practice. Great. After busting our butts helping to make this breakaway work, we now need to chase it down.

We'd better have a good reason for breaking the basic racing rule. We can't just chase our teammates willy-nilly. Bike racers get very upset when they look over their shoulder and see a matching jersey leading the chase without good cause.

NOT CAUGHT 'TIL IT'S CAUGHT

Bike racing offers two really strange phenomena that happen frequently. The first one is "Out of sight, out of mind." It's exactly as it sounds: When the breakaway gets a big enough lead, it will go around a corner and out of sight. Once it's out of sight, people forget about it, and the gap grows rapidly.

I know this sounds impossible. Surely, with the help of people along the course providing you with time splits, you can keep tabs on a breakaway and therefore keep it within range. But it is hard to chase after something you can't see. If you can't see it, you have no visual clue to how big the gap really is, and that lack of visual confirmation allows the gap to grow. Sounds crazy, but it's true. If it weren't, bike race announcers would never have reason to utter the phrase "Out of sight, out of mind."

The idea for the breakaway, then, is to get around a few turns as quickly as possible. Their biggest ally becomes diffidence on the part of the chasers.

That's not to say that once a breakaway is out of sight, it'll never be caught, but it certainly does happen a lot.

The other bizarre phenomenon is encapsulated in the bike racing phrase "It's not caught until it's caught."

If I had a dollar for every time I saw a breakaway come within a few feet of getting caught only to pull away again, I'd have about $37. It doesn't happen nearly as often as "Out of sight, out of mind," but it happens enough for me to tell you about it here. It happens when the chase effort relaxes just as it is about to make contact with the breakaway. Sometimes the gap will actually come down to a matter of feet between the wheels of the breakaway and the wheels of the chasers before the gap opens up again. It's not that the breakaway has sped up at the last minute. It's purely a result of the chasers assuming that their work is done when it actually isn't. Moments later, the gap grows again, and the chasers have difficulty reorganizing their chase.

You must drive that last nail into the coffin, or the vampire will escape again.

THE BREAK THAT LAPS THE FIELD

If you've done your job correctly, the breakaway containing your teammate(s) may eventually lap the field. When this happens, your team has a new task: Protect your rider.

When your teammate's breakaway is about to make contact from behind, send one or two riders to the back of the pack to greet him (Figure 5.5). The rules prevent you from dropping out of the pack to help the breakaway, but you are certainly permitted to wait at the back of the pack for contact to be made. When it's made, you must shepherd your teammate directly to the front of the field. Once there, be on the alert for more attacks.

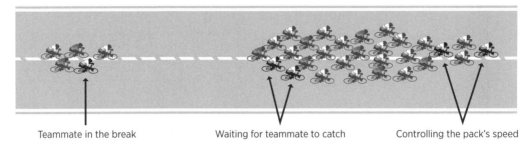

Teammate in the break   Waiting for teammate to catch   Controlling the pack's speed

FIGURE 5.5 Managing a lapped field

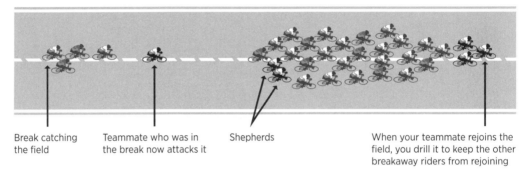

Break catching   Teammate who was in   Shepherds   When your teammate rejoins the
the field   the break now attacks it   field, you drill it to keep the other
                                                                breakaway riders from rejoining

FIGURE 5.6 Managing the field with a twist

The goal for your team is to keep your rider in contention at all times. Never let him or her fall asleep in the field. Don't let the other breakaway companions take off again without him. They'll probably try. In fact, you should attempt to launch your rider off the front again without the breakaway companions. If you're successful, your odds of winning will skyrocket.

Oftentimes, a rider who is in a breakaway that is about to lap the field will attack the breakaway well before contact is made (Figure 5.6). This gives him or her the advantage of slipping through the field and possibly off the front again. If that's your teammate, you can help in two ways: (1) lead him up through the field so that he's hidden from the wind, and (2) push the pace of the field so that the rest of his breakaway companions can't make contact.

Devious, no?

Conversely, if your teammate gets left behind short of lapping the field, you should send a few teammates to the front of the field to try to control the pace so that he has a better chance of making contact while a few more teammates wait at the back of the pack to bring him up to the front.

Your race is not over when a breakaway laps your field. When a breakaway rider that has lapped the field attacks again, go with him or her. It should be obvious that this rider is aggressive, strong, and determined. Those are qualities you look for in a breakaway companion. You would do well to join the attack.

Here's an interesting side note that I must make about lapping the field from the perspective of the breakaway riders: When you gain the lap and make contact with the field again, there is a cool feeling similar to the sensation of revisiting your high school when you're in college. The classes are easier. The hallways seem smaller. The kids are smaller. You've been working at a much higher level for a period of time, and it feels remedial to return to the group you graduated from.

The only way to get this feeling is to lap the field. Good luck.

DIVISION OF POWER

In amateur racing, there is a limited amount of power in any given field. Sure, everyone is fast, and everyone is capable and eager, but it's all relative. Some guys have really deep tanks. Some don't. Even in a field consisting solely of Cat. II riders, there will be different levels of ability within that group, and those different strata will become evident in the racing. Consequently, in whichever field we're discussing at any time, there is a limited number of riders who really possess the power to drive the pack, split the field, successfully break away, and possibly lap the field. (In the lower categories, they may have power but lack the wherewithal to break away.)

In that same field, there are several riders—in fact a majority of the field—who can hang with the fast group, and there are riders who will struggle late in the race when the pace really picks up.

If you're one of those "middle ground" riders who lacks the power to drive the break, you need to pay attention to the division of power among different groups. If you want to have a chance at winning prize money, you'll need to recognize where the power is located.

A comparison can be made to the college basketball power rankings. The top 10 NCAA teams will be favored in almost every game they play. Sure, they'll be upset now and again by a lesser team having a great game on the day when they are having a bad one. But they're ranked high for a reason and will win their share of games.

If you want to have a chance at winning prize money, you'll need to recognize where the power is located.

If a breakaway forms off the front containing 10 of the region's really fast guys, will there be enough horsepower left in the field to mount an effective chase effort? Or did all of the power go up the road? If so, that would be a great breakaway to bridge across to. Otherwise, say good-bye to a top-10 placing.

If you're able to get into a break containing a majority of the powerful riders, you just need to hold on for dear life and hope you don't get dropped. You're guaranteed a paying spot. Maybe. (I'll discuss this point later. You may not like it.)

If a breakaway forms containing a couple of "really fast guys" and a bunch of "kinda fast guys," then watch out for the next wave of attacks to come out of the peloton from the other really fast guys who missed the breakaway. They'll be reluctant to let the race get away from them.

If the field breaks into two or three different groups, you'll be able to guess the outcome by where the power is located. If you're in the third group and all the power is in the first or second group, your group will probably lack sufficient power to catch them.

Throughout the race, you must keep track of how deep the prize list goes and know where you are in relationship to the last paying spot. If, for instance, the race pays to the top 20 places, you need to know where that 20th place is at all times. Is it in front of you or behind you?

And if 20th place doesn't sound appealing, stick around. We're about to discover that the race isn't all about who comes in first.

6

WINNING AND OTHER LOFTY GOALS

WINNING THE RACE ISN'T EVERYONE'S GOAL, as I stated at the beginning, and it's not our team's only goal. We must also do what we can to cover other places in the results. As we're standing at the starting line waiting for the gun to go off, we can look around and assess the amount of power that's in the race. We'll know how deep the prize list goes. We can then estimate our payday potential.

If I show up with my team at a race that contains 20 of the best pros in the country, it's pretty easy to figure out how much money we won't be winning. Still, we race and we try.

It'll be fun no matter what. Always remember that.

Regardless of whether we win or lose, we must race for every placing as if it's first place.

In amateur racing, it's common to see a race end with a single breakaway followed by the main field. Amateur teams with riders in the break will often prevent any secondary breakaways that might threaten their leaders. Content with having placed a rider in the winning four-man break, they will block the field for the remainder of the race, and the field will sprint for fifth place.

What amateur racers sometimes fail to see in that scenario is that if four riders are up the road, then fifth place becomes the new first place and must be treated as such. If the breakaway has a secure lead, it's time to attack in an attempt to secure the next top placing. Not only that, but the same rules apply: Lead out the attack, get at least one of our teammates in the second break, be judicious in whom we let join the break, and block those who try to reel it in.

The goal here is simple: It's really nice to see a teammate listed in the results. But it's better to see several teammates listed in the results. If we can cash five prize checks instead of just one or two, we'll eat like kings! If creating a second group ensures that possibility, then we have to try.

And as soon as the second breakaway has a secure gap, we'll try for a third breakaway. We must do this until all places on the prize list are spoken for.

THE HUBER FLYER

If fifth place is the new first place, then it offers opportunities for riders who missed the breakaway. One of those opportunities is for the nonsprinters.

Chris Huber was a five-time U.S. Worlds Team member specializing in the individual pursuit in the late 1980s. He was untouchable at a distance of 3 kilometers. When he converted from trackie to roadie, he rode for the Coors Light Cycling Team, and he had a tactic that worked beautifully. I called it "the Huber Flyer."

With his team represented in the breakaway, Huber would sit in the main field and wait until the last three laps. As the sprinters began to fight for position at the front of the field, he would launch a scorching attack. If no one chased him, he would stay away until the finish, snatching the higher placing from the sprinters. If anyone chased him, Huber's teammates would quickly hop into that chaser's draft and use the chaser as their own personal lead-out man, thus setting themselves up beautifully for the sprint. If no one chased him, his sprinters were no worse off than before; they just had one less rider in their lead-out train.

Many times I watched the Coors Light team put four riders in the top six places by utilizing the Huber Flyer. It was a perfect team strategy that made use of Huber's strongest suit.

JOOP

Huber didn't use the Huber Flyer simply to mop up lower placings; he also used it to win races, but we didn't name that winning move after him. Instead, we named it after Joop Zoetemelk, the man who did it to perfection in the 1985 world championships. The 38-year-old Joop knew he stood no real chance against the younger sprinters who were bearing down on the finish line, so he attacked before the sprint started. Everyone watched him ride away but refused to take the initiative to chase after him. To them, it looked like a bungee attack, one that would soon come back to them. They didn't take it seriously. That's part of its charm. When it works, it can be a good day for the daring.

If you aren't blessed with sprinter's legs, your odds of beating the sprinters at their own game are pretty low. So you might as well try something foolish like a Joop attack.

One could argue that Zoetemelk took advantage of the egos of the other riders who refused to work with each other to bring back his attack. Luckily, we will never see this happen in our races because no egos exist at the amateur level. None at all. Nope. No egos here.

READING THE RACE

Bike racing is a thinking person's sport. There are so many decisions to be made during the course of the race, and they're influenced by many factors. Who is racing? What's the course profile? How do you feel? What just happened? What usually happens at this point on this course? What are the other teams doing?

Which teams are represented in the break? Who raced well last weekend and is on form to ride well again today? Is there one dominant rider? Is anything getting away today? How much horsepower is in the race? Is this a race that will be decided by attrition or a field sprint? How will the weather affect things? Are the same few guys doing all the work at the front? Who is hiding?

It's a matter not simply of predicting what will happen next but of anticipating all of the probabilities and having a corresponding response ready to use for each one.

Knowing, for example, who just expended energy, which teams have been active, who has been hiding, and what the road is like ahead will help you read the race and decide when to launch the withering attack that will etch your name in the history books.

I don't know if etching is necessary. Maybe you can just use a pen.

In many cases, reading a race means to simply be patient. More often, though, it means understanding the division or distribution of power. Where are the strong riders? What are they doing? Knowing who they are and what their tendencies are will allow you to react with the right amount of energy. You will be able to better decide whether to chase a certain breakaway or let it go and let others worry about it.

OVERFAMILIARITY

When we race against the same people every weekend, predictability becomes an issue. We can begin writing the script as we're watching who pulls into the parking lot. You can almost guess on which lap John will make his patented attack up the left side of the field. You probably know which five guys will be in the winning break, and you probably know who will win the field sprint. And your opponents can probably predict what you will do, too.

The key to breaking this routine is to either try new things or move to another part of the country, where everyone is new. Trying new things is less expensive.

If you're a sprinter, try a solo breakaway. Sure, some people may laugh at you, but remember that they laughed at Joop Zoetemelk. If you always attack on the hill, try attacking before the hill. If you always go on a solo attack from the gun, take a teammate and launch a two-man attack. Force the other teams to deal with something new.

Conversely, don't get lulled to sleep by the repetitive tactics of other teams. Just because they do the same thing every week doesn't mean they won't go off the page and try something they've never done before.

Think about what Thor Hushovd, a sprinter, did in the 2009 Tour de France. He launched a most unlikely solo attack on the mountainous stage 17. It's unthinkable for a sprinter to do such a thing. He remained solo over the next two climbs, the Col des Saisies and Cote d'Arâches. No one saw that one coming.

Practice things that make you a complete rider. Race to your strengths; train to your weaknesses.

Race to your strengths; train to your weaknesses.

You must also race to your opponent's weakness. If you aren't attacking a poor bike handler on a technical course or a weak climber on a big hill, you're writing him a free pass. Don't let him off the hook.

PATIENCE

After the race, when sitting in the parking lot discussing what went wrong, it's surprising how many times I hear racers wish they had been more patient in launching their sprint or responding to an attack. Surely the pressure that builds as the race progresses can cause some to jump the gun. Patience is a learned trait that comes with time and the realization that although we're hurtling toward the finish line like a bullet train, there's no need to rush things. Patience is what helps us stick to a plan and not react to every little blip along the way.

Patience also prevents you from giving up when all hope appears lost.

On the brick streets of Athens, Ohio, I once saw the perfect example of patience. Rain on bricks is a delightful combination; in this race, it shredded the peloton on the very first lap. Coors Light's criterium specialists, Roberto Gaggioli, Chris Huber, and Jonas Carney, took advantage of the chaos and quickly rode off the front. Meanwhile, the large pack fell apart like a cheap suit. It crumbled like Krakatoa. It exploded like . . . you get the idea. Within three slippery laps, it didn't look like much of a bike race. It looked like a charity ride with small groups scattered around the course except that three other riders had teamed up amid the melee of dropped riders. Subaru-Montgomery's Nate Reiss and Darren Baker teamed up with G.S. Mengoni's Radisa Cubric to form a second group that, despite being a half lap behind, slowly gained on the leaders.

The next hour of racing became an exciting team pursuit. Subaru-Montgomery had spent the season racing on cobbles in Europe. Coors Light had dominated the U.S. criterium circuit. Here, the two worlds collided.

The Subarus and Cubric were patient. They used the entire race to methodically work their way back into contention. They didn't try to do it all at once. They worked steadily to catch the Coors Light riders on the penultimate lap and eventually put two riders on the podium.

When reading a race and making decisions about which tactics to employ, the advantage will always go to the patient, clear thinking, level-headed warrior.

Please let me know what that's like.

WORKING THE BREAK

You made the break.

I assure you, your teammates are very proud of you right now. They will be happy to see you after the race. Specifically, after "payout."

How do you make the break work? Well, just remember how important cohesion and cooperation are to the synergy required to make a paceline run smoothly.

It's important to get that smooth rotation going as soon as possible. It requires short pulls on the front and a quick rotation to the back. There's no time to mess around. You've got 100 riders behind you wanting you to fail and working hard to make it happen. The first few minutes of a breakaway are ferocious and disorganized. Sometimes they require a leader.

When the breakaway begins working like a Swiss timepiece, it's magical. More often than not, however, it requires a little coaching. One rider sometimes needs to take the lead and direct the breakaway companions on when to pull through, how fast to pull through, and how fast to drop off, much like a coxswain on a rowing team tells the rowers at what tempo to pull the oars. That leader can be anyone. It might as well be you.

Chris Horner   RIDING IN THE BREAKAWAY

In the United States, the breakaway often requires someone to motivate the group and even tell other riders what to do—when to pull, how to pull, which direction to pull off, and so on. This seems to be quite a bit more common in the U.S. than in Europe. I would imagine that is mainly because most of the races in the U.S. at the pro level also have a lot of amateurs in the race, or at the very least many new pro riders who have passed through the amateur ranks so quickly that they have not yet learned the basics of bike racing.

It also isn't unusual for me to have to talk riders into doing some work in American pro races. Even at a race as big as the Tour of California, on the queen stage that finished on Mount Baldy in 2012, there was more talking than riding being done at times in the break. We had four RadioShack riders in the original break of 15 or 20 riders, which was

→

RIDING IN THE BREAKAWAY, CONTINUED

quickly down to 3 after using one of our riders to really get things going. Obviously, with Team RadioShack having the strongest riders in the break, the odds weren't great for the other guys. But even though they weren't the favorites, this was clearly going to be the break of the day, whether they worked or not. As I argued many times throughout the day, the more they worked, the larger the time gap would become and the more TV time they would get—not to mention at least some kind of chance for the win if we were to make it all the way to the finish.

As the stage continued, only about one-third of the break decided to work, and as a result, the time gap never grew big enough to give us a real chance to survive to the finish of the stage. At one point or another on the stage, everyone from the break was caught, with the last Colombian rider being swallowed up less than 1 km from the finish. I can't help but think that if only a few more riders, including the Colombian, had contributed throughout the stage, we would easily have been racing for the win instead of just the TV coverage. ◼

In the early stages of a breakaway, don't be afraid to be the whip, the guy who directs the paceline.

"We've got a gap," you shout. "Let's go. Short pulls. Everybody works!"

Once you're free from the field, start cracking the whip to make sure that everyone in your group is pulling on the oars with the same amount of intent. Don't assume that every rider in the group knows what he or she is doing. Some may be in the first breakaway of their career. They may appreciate your guidance. More to the point, they may need it.

Remember, you're not there to coach them. Your role as leader is to act as an ignition switch to get the motor started. Once it's running smoothly, the gap should grow, and you can shut up and figure out a way to beat them.

ROLL CALL

As your breakaway presses on toward the finish, you need to continually assess your companions and make sure that everyone is contributing evenly (Figure 6.1). Learn to read the other riders' faces to see if they're in pain or just pretending to be. If they aren't working, you need to find out to why. Are they indeed cooked? Are they along for a free ride? Or are they saboteurs intent on ruining the breakaway? Perhaps Miss Ohio?

There are a few tactics we can use to dissuade saboteurs, but it's difficult to overcome someone with devious intentions.

If the rider who refuses to contribute is indeed dead, then you must decide if you want to carry him and let him finish with a good result or, a less friendly option, get rid of him.

If you graciously decide to let him sit in and hang on for, say, fifth place in your five-man breakaway, what assurance do you have that he'll really accept your gift when the time comes? There's no guarantee that he won't sprint around you at the line. It's amazing how many riders seem to find their second wind in the final few miles of a race.

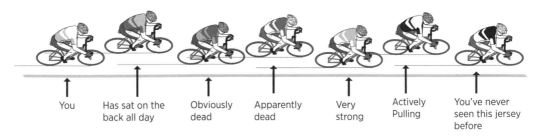

FIGURE 6.1 Roll call in the breakaway

In this kinder, gentler time we live in, it's likely that he is indeed telling the truth when he says he's cooked. I've heard stories of riders who sit on the back of a breakaway for the entire race, accept their gift, and then thank the rider who granted them the free ride. In the olden days, it was vastly different. Riders would make it their goal to get into a breakaway, do as little work as possible, and then sprint for the win even if they hadn't taken one pull throughout the entire race. There was no shame in that. The common thought of the day was that if the other riders weren't smart enough to figure out how to get rid of me, they didn't deserve to win. Or perhaps more correctly, if the other guys are stupid enough to let me sit on without working, they don't deserve to win.

So don't pull a wheelsucker all the way to the end and then get upset because he sprinted past you in the last few meters. Especially if he's wearing a kit from the 1980s.

If you're in a five-man breakaway with one rider who begs you to let him sit on for fifth place, think of this: You have teammates behind you currently fighting for sixth place. If you drop Mr. Deadwood, your teammates might get a higher placing.

That's how pro racers think.

GETTING RID OF THEM

Your first course of action when dealing with Mr. Deadwood should be to yell at him. Verbal razzing doesn't cost anything energy-wise. It may be enough to get him to contribute. It's sure worth a try. You can do this as kindly or unkindly as you like. Anything said in a bike race is exempt from most local bullying laws and is usually forgotten during the cooldown ride after the race. Don't worry about insulting every aspect of his life. He'll get over it.

Another plan for getting rid of the deadwood is to attack. At the very least, push the pace. Only the strong survive. If he's really cooked, he'll have difficulty

Freeloader   You

FIGURE 6.2 Gapping someone out of a breakaway

responding. If he's able to respond, then he should be able to contribute. Feel free to yell at him again.

If attacking or yelling doesn't work, try this: As you drop to the rear of the paceline, Mr. Deadwood will likely open up a little gap in front of him and allow you the privilege of slipping in front of him, thus preventing him from ever rotating to the front (Figure 6.2). When you get in front of him, slow down. A lot. Allow a huge gap to open in front of you. Let it grow as large as you can. Wait for Mr. Deadwood to jump around you to close the gap. If he wants to stay with the breakaway, he'll eventually decide to go around you. When he goes past you, jump on his wheel and let him tow you back up to the group.

This is a complex tactic that requires a unified effort by everyone in the breakaway to help out. If you're the only one who's concerned about the freeloader, this tactic will not work.

All riders in the breakaway must do the same thing to Mr. Deadwood every time they rotate to the back. That is, take him off the back and make him chase to regain contact. This requires him to work very hard to stay in the break, or die trying. Not literally, of course. We don't want anyone to die in pursuit of a pair of socks and a TGI Fridays gift card.

This tactic is effective but extremely rare in the amateur ranks. It relies on every rider knowing how to successfully gap another rider and have the strength to survive in the process. Most riders in a breakaway are at their limit already.

Well, some are.

SHOULD I STAY OR SHOULD I GO?

When is your breakaway done? When is the party over? Or to put it another way, when are you no longer required to do any work?

Each time you look over your shoulder, you see the field getting a little closer. (Personally, I'm always a wee bit flattered when my breakaway is chased down and reeled in. I feel respected, as if they saw me as some sort of threat.)

At some point it will become apparent to you that the end is near. You're going to be caught; it's just a matter of time. Still, you can't just apply the brakes and drop back to the field. You must continue to try because you just never know what's going to happen.

Earlier I told you about the phenomenon called "It's not caught until it's caught." I wasn't kidding. You are still considered a breakaway until the chasers make contact with you. If you're cooked, give up. It's pointless to go on. But if you have any life left in you, make them catch you. Don't slow down and wait for them. They may, as incredible as it may seem, lose their focus. Or perhaps your teammates will put up an impenetrable force field. And you'll find the gap growing again.

But that's rare. Usually you're caught, and your dreams are squashed. So get over it, and be on the lookout for the next attack.

In fact, you can go one better. Go on the attack yourself. During those last few moments of your dying breakaway, drink some water, rest the legs, take in some big gulps of air, and launch your attack while you still have a bit of a gap. You'll find that a couple of things can happen.

1. You might get caught right away. That's OK; nothing ventured, nothing gained. You never know until you try.
2. You might get away. You see, every now and then, the field will see that the breakaway is caught, and they'll relax just a wee bit. It's as if they're pausing to reflect on their successful chase efforts.

In that moment of hesitation, while they're patting themselves on the back, your attack may catch them off guard. That gap that they just closed will open up again, and they may not be ready to go back to work.

Here's a really odd analogy: After dinner, you've just washed all the dishes in the kitchen. Everything is finally put away. You're happy with how clean your kitchen looks. And then your kid brings you a bowl of half-eaten Cheerios that's been in his bedroom for a week.

You take the bowl, throw it into the sink, turn out the lights, and walk away. You'll get it later.

That's what I'm talking about. You just did all that work. You thought you were done, and you're not ready for more.

It happens in bike racing, too.

7

SPRINTING

SPRINTING ISN'T SIMPLY A DRAG RACE between the fastest riders in the race. Nor is it simply a test of brute strength and fearlessness. It's much more than that.

The finish line is approaching. By this point in the race, you should have sized up your competition. You should know which teams and riders will be a factor in the outcome. Now it's time to consider all of the other variables that will play a part.

KNOW YOUR RANGE

Are you willing to stick your nose into the fray and bump elbows with other riders at 30 mph? If all attempts to break away have failed and you still have ambitions of winning, you're going to have to mix it up in a pack sprint involving everyone, whether they are contenders or not. Even if you're in the leading breakaway and you have ambitions of winning, you're going to have to sprint for it (albeit with fewer flailing elbows coming at you).

Heck, even if 16th place appeals to you more than 17th place, you're going to have to sprint for it.

Earlier in the book, I urged you to work on bike-handling skills. I told you about getting out of the saddle smoothly, holding a straight and predictable line, and not overreacting to movements near you. I hope you've been working on all of those skills because the need for them is magnified during a sprint.

There are many variables to consider when talking about sprinting. And since you haven't skipped ahead to the next section by now, I'll assume that you fancy yourself a sprinter (as opposed to, say, a climber or a time trialist or a rouleur). Or maybe you're just sprinter-curious.

First of all, here's an understatement: All sprinters are not created equal. You probably already knew that.

The good ones possess many similar characteristics, but there's more to sprinting than just being fast and fearless.

First, you must know your maximum effective range. If you were a bullet fired from a gun, how far could you travel with enough velocity to penetrate a cantaloupe? You don't want simply to reach the cantaloupe/finish line; you want to carry your maximum speed through it. So how far can you hold your top speed on flat terrain?

You need to know your range precisely. If, for example, your range is 150 meters, don't begin your sprint 300 meters from the finish line. You will fall harmlessly to the ground short of the melon.

You'll also need to know how wind and the course finish affect your range. Obviously a headwind or a climb to the finish will shorten your range; a tailwind or a descent will make it longer.

WHAT'S YOUR SPEED?

The first car I ever owned was a 1977 Ford Thunderbird. It was a dog off the line, but it had a high top end and could go from 50 to 100 mph quickly. My neighbor had a 1978 Pontiac Firebird that could jump off the line and get to 100 mph without much effort at all. (This was before the 1979 energy shortage ruined all cars forever.) So if we were to race away from a stoplight, I had no chance. But if we were already rolling, I could hold my own quite nicely. That is, if we were racing our cars on public roads, which is totally illegal, dangerous, and ill-advised.

Are you a Thunderbird or a Firebird? Do you prefer a sprint that starts at a lower speed or a higher speed? In other words, can you jump to hyperspeed from a complete standstill? Or do you need to be rolling at a good clip before you go supersonic? This is one way in which sprinters differ.

In a field sprint, you will have no choice in the matter. The pack will drive toward the finish line with the same sense of urgency as subway passengers trying to catch the last train: rudely fast. As a result, you will have to sprint from a fast pace unless your teammates can control the pace in the last mile of the race.

In a small breakaway group, however, you may be able to exert some control over the pace in the final kilometer so that you can start your sprint from a speed that you prefer. If you don't control it, then some other rider or riders will dictate the speed at which the sprint starts. If you sprint best from a slower speed, you need to learn how to be the dictator.

> *The pack will drive toward the finish line with the same sense of urgency as subway riders trying to catch the last train.*

Here's one way: In the last kilometer, go to the front of your small breakaway group and treat it as if you're blocking for a teammate who is up the road. Ease up on the throttle. They'll probably let you. Few riders will wish to show initiative on the front of the group in the final kilometer. If no one comes around you to take over the lead, you can continue to drop your speed. Try to hide your excitement, and be ready to jump. Pick your moment, and go hit the cantaloupe.

If, however, you sprint best starting at a higher pace and find yourself in a small group, you may need to be the one to push the pace as you get closer to the line. You're driving a Ford Thunderbird, so you can't afford to let the pace dip too low. Meanwhile, other riders will gladly sit in your draft and work 30 percent less than you at this point in the race. I sure would.

By sitting on the front, though, you risk becoming the carrot that is dangled in front of the horse's mouth. Pick a speed that is purposeful but not fatiguing. As the distance to the finish clicks down, you can expect a counterattack that will come around you at high speed. At that point, you have to be ready to throw it into higher gear. Luckily, you saved something for that.

Another tactic is to make fake attacks from the second or third position. Don't go all out; just go fast enough to keep the pace up and toy with the nerves and emotions of the other riders. Strike fear into their hearts by making them think the sprint is beginning. Your only intention is to keep the pace high, but they don't know that. They think you're trying to attack. Eventually someone will become nervous or impatient, and they'll likely launch a real attack too early, thus pushing the pace up to your preferred launch speed. You will get in their draft and wait until you reach your perfect range.

You also must know your optimum cadence for reaching and holding your maximum speed. Some people are comfortable spinning a high cadence. Some like to mash a big gear at a low cadence. Practice your sprint until you know exactly which gear suits your sprinting motor.

These are tactics that require a lot of experimentation that you need to conduct during group training rides and in your individual interval training.

MEASURING DISTANCE: RECON THE COURSE

As you reconnoiter the course, you must measure the final 200 meters and make sure you know where it starts. If the course isn't marked, look for some prominent feature by the side of the road and make a mental note of it. Two hundred meters is the standard benchmark distance in cycling by which every sprinter measures his or her sprint. It's also the distance in which the rules change to accommodate fairness in sprinting. It doesn't mean that you must

Chris Horner   FIRST GUY INTO THE LAST CORNER

With sprinting not being one of my strongest cycling abilities, my preference during any race was always to get away in a break to avoid the field sprint altogether and increase my own chances for the win. But if that wasn't possible, and if we had no sprinter on the team who had a good chance to win the race, my next-best option was always to be the first guy into the last corner.

I know it sounds strange, but every guy in the field wants to come into the last corner near the front but not on the front. They want to stay out of the wind so that they can save energy for the final few hundred meters. As a result, the fight for any position other than the first wheel is always the most dangerous to be in on the last lap, unless of course you have an amazing lead-out train.

By putting yourself into the corner first, there's less chance of being crashed because you never have anyone next to you—and none of the guys behind you can say that. With each position behind first, the field gets wider and wider, with more guys fighting to get through the last corner, all side by side.

Now, of course there's also a downside—otherwise everyone would want to be there! The problem with coming through the corner first is that if the finish line is more than 250 meters from the corner, you have basically zero chance of winning since everyone behind you is getting a free ride. But when you have my kind of speed, I'm always going to get passed anyway, and the only real question is by how many. Either way, the odds of winning are not high, so I always thought that it was better to be passed by a few more guys at the finish than not to make it to the finish at all. ◼

start your sprint 200 meters from the finish. It's only a guidepost to help you determine where you need to unleash your sprint based on your maximum effective range.

Here's an example of how a pro racer thinks: If I am in my 53x15, it is exactly 27 revolutions from the 200-meter point to the finish line.

Pro racers know measurements like that, and they know how to count them off in the final sprint.

For your purposes, you also need to note how far the finish line is from the final corner, how tight the corner is, and how the run-up to the final corner is laid out. Those three points will tell you a lot about how the race will end. If it's a long finishing stretch, you may have enough room to allow you to be the fifth or sixth rider out of the final turn and still have a chance to win the race. If the finishing stretch is short, you may need to be the first rider out of the final turn to have a chance of winning. If so, then the real sprint will actually occur on the back side of the course as riders try to be the first rider into the final turn. What if you're the second rider through the final turn? Do you still have time to pass the leader?

Here's a tip that will help you in this situation. As you steam toward the final turn sitting in second position, allow a small gap to open between you and the rider in front (Figure 7.1). As you approach the final turn, you should accelerate into that gap and carry more speed through the corner. Cut the turn a little sharper so that you pass the leader on the inside. If you go to the outside, the leader can swing wide and pin you against the outside curb. If you hesitate for an instant, you will lose your momentum, and you'll give away the win.

The famous criterium course in Downers Grove, Illinois, had eight turns and a hill, but the most decisive feature was the final turn. It was the tightest turn on the course and just 125 meters from the finish line. To have a chance at winning a race on that course, you needed to be in the top two positions as you came out of that turn. As a result, the real sprint took place just before the turn, and big crashes took place in that turn. As a sprinter on that course, the

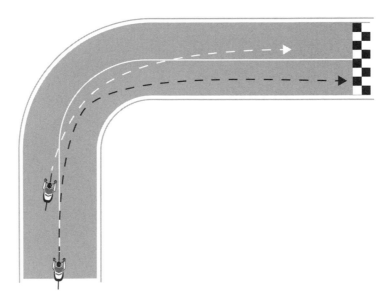

FIGURE 7.1 Let a gap form before the final corner so you can accelerate through the inside of the turn.

game began much earlier, and the eight corners on the course made it a challenging game.

Watching other races on the course before you race your event will help you figure out where you need to be as you go through the final turn on the last lap.

Note whether there is a wind and what the terrain looks like at the finish; think about the effect those conditions will have on the pack when it swings out of the final turn.

You'll need to know all of this in order to time your jump. There's nothing quite like the feeling of jumping out of the draft into a wall of wind and finding yourself going backward.

POSITIONING

One of the worst things that can happen during a sprint is to get boxed in. One of the best things that can happen is to have your rivals get boxed in.

Eddy Gragus won the USPRO championship in 1996 mainly because he noticed that his rivals' front wheels were on the wrong side of the rear wheels of other riders. In other words, everyone else was locked in. So when Eddy jumped in the final 500 meters, no one could respond quickly enough. That brief hesitation was enough to create a gap that he held all the way to the podium.

It is nearly impossible to plan on something like that happening. You can only be ready to capitalize on it when you see it. However, you can be smart enough to make sure it doesn't happen to you. That comes from watching the movement of the pack and predicting what it will do to your position. You must also commit to your plan of being in a certain position at a specific point of the race, and be patient enough to allow the sprint to develop.

Chris Horner   THE EDDY GRAGUS ATTACK

During the 1996 USPRO championship, the Postal Service team had four riders in the break, and if I remember correctly, no other team had more than one. The Postal guys were attacking us left and right, all the way to the finish. As we went into and started to exit the last roundabout before the final straightaway, Eddy Gragus was the only one of the four who hadn't been attacking throughout the day. He had been sitting on and resting, if you can call it that, during the entire length of the breakaway. I can't remember which position I was in, but I was somewhere near the front—maybe fifth or sixth wheel—when Gragus came flying by on the inside of the roundabout just as we were exiting.

It was a beautiful move, and one that was perfectly timed because not only were all of our wheels overlapped to the outside of the turn as

→

The next plateau of sprinting and positioning is to do something that NASCAR drivers do: slingshot. In stock-car racing, to "slingshot" means to take a run at the back end of the car in front of you and use the slipstream as a way to get more speed to pass or attack. In cycling, we use the word "slingshot" to mean using momentum to launch a sprint or to launch an attack.

To slingshot properly, you first open up a small gap between you and the rider in front of you. Be careful not to make it appear obvious. If people behind you are hip to what you're doing, they will try to zoom past you and fill the gap. (I certainly would.) Next, accelerate into the gap and feel the vacuum of the draft pull you right past the rider. As you pass him, you will be accelerating while he is still riding at the same tempo. He is already behind and is therefore playing catch-up. And the riders who were behind you didn't get the same advantage of the vacuum. They are playing catch-up, too.

THE EDDY GRAGUS ATTACK, CONTINUED

he attacked on the inside, but it was also impossible to follow his move on the left side because the road narrowed as we were entering the final straightaway, closing off the left side of the road. When we entered the straightaway, Gragus already had a sizable gap, so whichever rider went after him first would certainly be sacrificing any chance of winning the USPRO jersey. I had Roberto Gaggioli in front of me, who at the time was one of the fastest racers on the domestic scene. I was certain he or one of the other fast guys in the group was going to chase Gragus down, but in the end we were all probably thinking the same thing. As the seconds of hesitation ticked by, we all got a front-row seat to watch Eddy Gragus ride away with the USPRO championship. ◼

LEAD-OUT

When it comes to the actual sprint, much is said about the lead-out train. We see it used to the fullest in the pro races in which the teams are lined up like ribbons as the peloton enters the final 10 kilometers. The general idea is that each team will deliver its sprinter to the finish line by performing a very fast paceline that rotates only once. The guy on the front pulls off and quits. The next guy pulls through, pulls off, and quits. And so on. If all goes according to plan, the final lead-out rider will begin his big push about 500 to 600 meters from the line. The sprinter will then decide when it's time to launch his final kick, usually at about 200 meters or so.

That's the theory, anyway. In amateur races, the chaos of the final kilometers often plays as big a role in the outcome. Having a strong team of riders driving the lead-out train is important, but the real issues are timing and finding a clear path to the finish line. Lacking those, you are destined to cash the smaller check.

While working as an announcer at amateur races, I have often seen teams try to conduct the lead-out train using five or six riders lined up in front of their designated sprinter. They'll often take the extra precaution of positioning one rider behind the sprinter to act as a blocker to prevent other teams from latching on to the sprinter's rear wheel. They'll amass near the front of the pack in the final kilometers and dutifully ramp up the pace.

Sometimes it works. Sometimes it doesn't.

It's not an easy tactic for an amateur team to pull off successfully, as it requires an equal level of ability among all team members. If one rider lets a gap open in the train by going either too fast or too slow, it falls apart. Thus, while it may seem obvious to call on every rider on your team to help with the lead-out, in fact it is better to call just upon those who have the legs to pull it off. Riders who have cooked themselves throughout the race may not have anything left in the final mile and therefore shouldn't even try to mix it up in

Chris Horner   GEARING UP FOR THE SPRINT

I've been a professional for 19 years, and every year, whether I have changed teams or not, the chemistry of riders within the team changes. Some teams, like the Mercury team, had a lead-out train that was so well oiled that we never had to speak with one another before the finish of every field sprint. Everyone knew his role within the train and did his part to deliver our sprinter to the line.

Then of course there have been others that were not so well oiled. This is where I've seen a big difference between the U.S. teams and the European teams. Many times people talk about how the Europeans do everything so much stronger, faster, and better in general in the sport of cycling, but I've often seen that when it comes to the sprints, the lead-out trains in the U.S. are easily as well developed, if not more so, than most of those in Europe. My theory is that all of the criteriums we do allow us much more practice in getting our timing and positioning right.

Certainly my favorite team for lead-outs had to be the Mercury team. We had multiple sprinters on Mercury, but our go-to sprinter was always Gord Fraser. In 100 lead-outs, I'm pretty certain he won 99 times.

The lead-out normally happens in a criterium no sooner than 10 laps to go. Even 10 can be a little far from the finish, but certainly if the team is strong and well oiled, I've seen it done successfully from that far out and have been part of doing it many times.

It always starts the same, with the guys with less speed in their legs rotating for the first four or five laps. This is when it can get a little tricky. With five laps to go, the speed has to be picked up to a point where no one is capable of attacking and where you hope no other team is

→

GEARING UP FOR THE SPRINT, CONTINUED

organized enough or strong enough to be able to pass. At this point, the whole team is rotating with the exception of your last lead-out man, and of course your sprinter. If you have a really strong team, it is possible to even have a third guy who won't have to do any work until you are under half a lap to go.

As the team enters the last lap, each teammate takes his final pull. This should be his all-in effort, throwing everything at it until he explodes with nothing left in his legs. If he's really experienced, it wouldn't be strange for him to cause a little havoc on the other teams behind on his way backward through the group. With all of the early workers spent, this is the point when the lead-out man, who has (ideally) been sitting on for the entire race, starts his sprint. His job is to get his sprinter to at least the last corner safely in the lead, where the finish line should be just a few pedal strokes away. In a perfect world, the sprinter finishes it off and the team rolls away with another win in the bag. ▪

the lead-out train. They need to let their teammates know that they're toast before crunch time comes.

You must also be careful to hold your line throughout the sprint. If you are providing a lead-out to your teammate, do not swing off to one side dramatically when your job is done. This swashbuckling move is a guaranteed crash-maker. Instead, just pull slightly to one side, continue to ride a straight line, and allow the riders behind you to pick their safe line past you. If you're sprinting and your engine sputters out, don't try to get out of the way. Just hold your line and have faith that the riders behind you are looking forward as they're supposed to.

FORM

As far as technique is concerned, think of the Jim Furyk golf swing.

Jim Furyk is a great PGA Tour golfer famous for his very unorthodox swing, which has won a U.S. Open, a FedEx Cup Championship, and the Vardon Trophy. Television broadcasters advise young children to look away when Jim Furyk is about to hit the ball lest they pick up bad habits. (If winning the U.S. Open is a bad habit, I want it.)

There's no law that says you have to look like everyone else when you sprint, but you'll probably discover why most sprinters have a similar (though not identical) style. To develop your own sprint, you need to experiment with your weight distribution, gear selection, cadence, the use of your upper body, and combinations thereof. Your sprint will be as unique as your signature. You will find the sweet spot in which you can make the bike go its fastest (preferably with you on it). Once you do, practice, practice, practice.

Here are eight key elements of successful sprinting style:

1. Don't pitch yourself too far forward over your front wheel. If you are hanging off the front of your bike, your rear wheel may tend to bounce and skip around. This will rob you of power.
2. Don't be too far back, either. If you position your weight too far to the rear, you will not have the best grip on your steering or leverage on your handlebars.
3. Your hands should be on the drops. Your grip should be airtight. You do not want to let go now.
4. You must sprint in a straight line. Your bike may waggle and your body may sway, but you must commit to a line and stay on it.
5. You need to be clipped in like nobody's business. Please inspect your pedals and cleats periodically. On behalf of every other sprinter near you, I thank you in advance.

6. Keep your head up and your eyes open. Do not fixate on your front wheel.

7. Watch for riders who have stopped sprinting. They will appear to be moving backward. Anticipate this. It should never surprise you.

8. Never throw your hands in the air to celebrate your victory until after you cross the finish line. Ignore this advice and you may go viral on YouTube.

When it comes to unleashing your thunderous sprint that distorts the fabric of time, you must bring all of these ideas together. And let's add one more thing: the killer instinct. To be a great sprinter, you need to want it in a way that pretty much blinds you to everything else. You need desire, and you need absolute belief in your skills.

If your heart isn't in it 100 percent, you should probably reconsider your sporting choices. Sprinting takes commitment.

COMMUNICATION

With all that's happening in a bike race, communication with your teammates is critical. A team must practice communicating if its members are serious about enacting team tactics and winning races.

How do you share observations about other riders without broadcasting them to everyone within earshot? How do you tell your lead-out train that you're not having a good day when you're sitting at the back of the pack? How do you know who is in the breakaway and how big the gap is? How do you spread the word when you're scattered throughout the field? What information really needs to be shared?

Communication issues were completely resolved with the advent of race radios in the peloton. Radios allowed teammates to talk to one another. They allowed a team director to move his riders around like chess pieces, giving real meaning to the term "rolling chess game." This made for safer racing by allowing for instant warnings of upcoming course hazards. Unfortunately, radios also removed a lot of the thinking and guesswork that was a part of bike racing.

Their use has since been banned in amateur races, placing the emphasis on verbal communication and nonverbal signals among teammates at race speed—not an easy task.

I've already mentioned that frantic arm waving is a popular method for alerting your teammates that something's wrong. It only works if they can actually see you, can understand what it means, and actually care.

For example, one universal signal seen in bike racing is when one teammate at the front of the field looks over his shoulder and gives the "we missed the breakaway again because y'all were asleep; now, c'mon up and help me chase, damnit" signal to his teammates. It consists of frantic arm waving similar to the gesticulating of a third base coach waving a baseball runner home. It is usually given with an air of frustration.

For more intricate messages, it's helpful to have a nonriding teammate or coach positioned along the course to relay information to the riders. This is a valuable addition to a team riding in any multilap event. It's almost completely worthless in a point-to-point road race.

To make the course-side information system work, it's important to keep the messages short and to the point. A succinctly worded shout from the road-side can be a very helpful thing. However, a wordy diatribe will only serve as a demonstration of the Doppler effect.

For example, my teammate, Ray Dybowski, was once on a solo breakaway in Sanford, Florida, on a boulevard course with two 180-degree turns. As he came through one of the turns, his friend Joe Saling yelled at him. On the next lap, Joe yelled again with what Ray was sure were valuable instructions. Though it was difficult at race pace to hear Joe and hard to comprehend what he was saying, Ray understood Joe this way: "The key is to put more weight on the front wheel. Don't reach!"

Ray started leaning forward in the turns and found he had better traction and was able to carry more speed through the corners. He eventually won the race and excitedly thanked Joe for the advice afterward. Joe was perplexed. He hadn't shouted any instructions. He was trying to tell Ray, "We left the keys to the car on the front wheel. We couldn't wait. We're going to the beach."

In my many years of racing, I've come to a few conclusions about roadside coaches.

- They should stand on an uphill section where they'll have more time to convey messages to the riders, or on a high point where they can see a good portion of the course.
- They should stand away from the crowd and the announcers. Those announcers are just so annoying. All they do is yammer. Nobody listens to what they're saying, anyway.
- They should stay in the same place throughout the entire race. Their riders shouldn't have to look for them every lap.
- They should do more than simply announce the time gap each lap. That information is almost entirely useless unless there's a chase effort in which riders need to know if they're gaining or losing ground.

I've come to admire team managers such as Mike Tamayo of the United Healthcare Pro Cycling Team, who can relay everything his riders need to know by using gestures (see page 164, "The Subtle Art of Hand Gestures").

His effectiveness at communicating in the simplest manner comes from the experience of working together as a team every weekend. It's difficult to communicate as elegantly without practice.

A more common scenario at the lower amateur levels is to complain to your teammates all the way home because so-and-so didn't do what we talked about before the race. This isn't because so-and-so is a slacker but because his rear derailleur wasn't shifting properly and he couldn't get to the front. But you wouldn't know that because Mike Tamayo wasn't alongside the course flashing you the "so-and-so is out of the picture" signal.

Chris Horner RACE RADIOS

For many years now, the UCI has been trying to eliminate race radios altogether. My personal opinion on the subject is that race radios are way too important to the safety of the riders and to the knowledge of what's happening in the race to allow them to be banned. To do away with the radios would leave us without the knowledge of how far away the break is, whom we are actually chasing (who is in the break), and, of course, warnings about dangerous turns or road debris that we may be coming up on at very fast speeds. It is true that each team director is giving orders to his or her riders, but in the end, it is always the rider himself who needs to make the decision on the road as to how he is going to race the bike, and the information he gets through the race radio helps him make that decision.

One time (OK, maybe three or four times) I crashed into a very deep ditch where I could not be seen by the caravan of director cars or officials as they passed by. At that point, the only way that I knew someone was aware of my predicament, being upside down and tangled up in my bike while still clipped into the pedals, was by using my race radio to tell my director where to start looking for me. Who knows, maybe without a radio I'd still be in that ditch waiting for someone to come help untangle me! ◼

THE *Subtle Art* OF HAND GESTURES

 Bringing his hands together slowly as if clapping in slow motion: **The gap is coming down.**

Moving his hands apart as if he is lying about the size of a fish he caught: **The gap is growing.**

Twirling his finger as if to say he's heard this story before: **Pick up the pace.**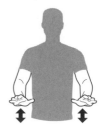

 Showing both palms: **Keep it steady.**

Bouncing a ball with both hands: **Back it off.**

If you drop out of your race before it ends, you can do your teammates a favor if you remain next to the course and help supply them with information rather than simply going back to the car to change your clothes. Cycling is a team sport, and you're still on the team whether you're on the saddle or on the curb.

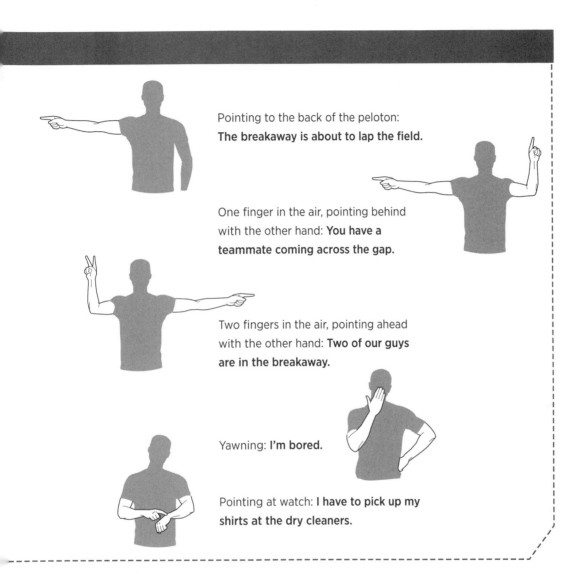

Pointing to the back of the peloton:
The breakaway is about to lap the field.

One finger in the air, pointing behind
with the other hand: **You have a
teammate coming across the gap.**

Two fingers in the air, pointing ahead
with the other hand: **Two of our guys
are in the breakaway.**

Yawning: **I'm bored.**

Pointing at watch: **I have to pick up my
shirts at the dry cleaners.**

The advantage of having a roadside coach is that he or she can make more
accurate observations standing in one place than you can from your bike in the
peloton. A coach can more accurately tell you where the power distribution is
and can provide the names of riders in the breakaway, where you may be just

guessing. A coach will also know where every one of your teammates is located in the pack and can tell them where they need to be.

The answer to that last one is pretty simple: at the front.

GET ON MY WHEEL

We often talk about the unspoken moments when things just fall into place, such as a rotating paceline. Here are some other moments that should fall under this heading.

Get on my wheel. We're moving up. Now. If a teammate moves toward the front, don't just watch him ride past you. Take that as your invitation to get on his wheel and go with him. It's a free ride. As I stated before, it is rarely a bad idea to move forward. You don't have to go straight to the front, but you can at least improve your position at little cost to your own energy stores.

My breakaway just got caught, and another attack just went. Go with it. Now. If you're in any sort of position to attack when your teammate's breakaway gets caught, it's optional. If another attack transpires in the meantime, your response is mandatory. Don't wait for your teammate to yell at you to go with it. Just go.

Our teammate just got in a promising breakaway. Get your butt up to the front. Now. Unless your name is Tyler Farrar and your only job is to sit in the back of the pack and wait for the final 200 meters, you are expected to be at the front of the pack to help block when your team is represented in a breakaway, promising or otherwise.

Our team missed the breakaway. We need to chase it down. Go to the front and hammer. Don't count on getting any help from any other team. The people you're racing against are lazy sheep. They will look around for someone else to take the initiative. There's no time to waste in beginning the chase effort.

Our teammate's breakaway is about to lap the field. Go to the back of the pack. Wait for the breakaway. Escort your teammate to the front. Keep your eyes open for another attack by the other breakaway riders. Their new goal is to drop their breakaway companions. Your goal is to protect your teammate from this happening.

We're in the final mile; let's get the train started. The race is a rush forward, always. Seldom will you be asked by your teammates to go backward when the finish line is in sight. If you have a sprinter on your team, your position is waiting for you somewhere in front of him. You've worked on this and have perfected it. It's time to break the hearts of the lazy sheep by showing them how you win a sprint.

Occasionally you may have to go backward to find your sprinter and escort him to the front. That's about the only reason to go backward in the final miles.

Our team strongman just flatted. Without him, we are doomed. This one isn't an unspoken moment. It will happen when a team member makes the discovery and alerts the others.

Some of your teammates should drop out of the pack and wait for the strongman or strongwoman and help tow them back to the pack. Meanwhile, the others should go to the front and control the pace so that it's easier to catch up.

COMBINES

A breakaway requires an otherwise unlikely cooperation between opponents. Without it, a breakaway would never happen.

Even more interesting than the cooperation in a breakaway, however, are the cooperative agreements or verbal contracts we often form with nonteammates to ensure that we have help in a race. Forming an ad hoc team with opponents is a rare phenomenon in sport. It is something that we see in the upper categories of amateur racing, but not so much in the lower ranks. Allow me to explain.

On any given weekend throughout the summer, there are dedicated bike racers living as vagabonds, traipsing from town to town in search of a cash prime or a top-10 placing to help pay for their bohemian lifestyle. Their territory may be the entire country, or it may be a five-state area. They travel with like-minded riders from other teams. Come race time, these traveling gypsies will band together to form a team while wearing an assortment of jerseys.

Or they may recruit helpers when the racing is under way, thus creating a team in as few as three elementary sentences:

1. "You got any teammates with ya?"
2. "No, you?"
3. "No. Let's work together."

This conversation may take place during the race or in the parking lot before the race. It's usually held between two or three people. It's a conversation that's short enough to have while waiting at the start line. But most importantly, the fact that this conversation takes place at all is testament to the fact you're better off with teammates.

This arrangement is called a "combine," and it's often formed with riders with whom you're at least somewhat familiar. However, that's not a requirement. But one thing you all need know is what your strengths are.

Them asking you, "Do you have a sprint?" implies that they don't.

You saying to them, "Let's go!" implies that you're going to attack together.

Them saying to you, "Go with that one" implies that you're to join a break-away. The inference is that they will block for you, and you'll share whatever winnings you're able to muster.

No contracts get signed. No secret handshake takes place. You just wing it wearing different jerseys. It's those mismatched jerseys that make this union unique. Since you don't match, you'll attract less attention. Other teams will be slow to pick up on your collusion if they notice it at all. Few riders will suspect that you're in cahoots with one another.

Here's a strange example: I was racing in a criterium in Lansing, Michigan. I happened to be very near the front of the pack (trust me; I'm just as surprised as you are by this) when a four-man breakaway formed off the front. It quickly established a gap, and it was time for me to decide whether I was going to bridge across to it. I looked at the riders in front of me and saw that one rider was blocking very effectively, though he had no teammate in the breakaway.

As we came out of a hard right-hand turn, I noticed that he slowly pinched the front of the field against the left curb, bringing our speed down by about 4 mph. Well played.

"Hmm," I thought, "that's odd. He's going to great lengths to make sure this breakaway succeeds, yet his own team missed it completely."

Actually, at the time I thought something much less civilized than that.

Then I realized that his brother-in-law was in the breakaway. His brother-in-law rides for another team.

Cahoots.

When it comes to combines, there is little to say and not much time to say it, which is why we see this occur more in the upper categories. Needless to say, a lot of assumptions are made when this union is formed. For instance, riders who form combines can assume that a rider knows everything I wrote in the first half of this book.

That's one of many cool things about it.

Chris Horner   DEALS MADE WITH RIVALS

Deals made with nonteammates are a possibility in just about any race you enter, but they are especially common at smaller races where the pro teams may not be showing up in full force. I have always looked for the possibility of a combine whenever one of the best sprinters in the race was arriving without any teammates. For sure, he was going to seek help from other riders to control the race all the way to the finish and to help him take the win. At one particular criterium event, I saw five riders from three different teams all working together in a combine.

The most memorable combine in my career was during the Tour of Southland in New Zealand. At one point during the race, while our team had the race leader's jersey with Eric Wohlberg, at least five other teams formed a combine against us to take the jersey. It was such a masterful combine that everyone involved must have been talking about how to orchestrate it the night before, as amazingly enough even the race radios from the officials weren't working properly, making it impossible to know the time gaps between the field and the breakaway riders. The main reason that this particular combine was so difficult for me to predict was because it had nothing to do with personal results or prize money, only national pride: All the riders in the combine were from New Zealand. Their entire race was dedicated to making sure that a foreigner didn't come in and steal their home race out from under them.

Later that night, before the second stage of the day started, all of the details of the plan were leaking out. My team was so upset after finding out what had happened that we went on a rampage during the next stage, where no one was safe. The amount of handlebar smashing and aggressive riding from my team during the race was unlike anything I had ever witnessed before or since, but I think we made our point. ■

PICKING THE RIGHT STRANGERS

We've finally found something that bike racing shares with the fine art of square dancing: You can choose your partner.

But choose wisely and measure your efforts. It's just like any other relationship. There are givers, and there are takers.

Forming a combine is not the result of complex decisions. It's whomever you wrangle in the parking lot, really. The whole idea is to just have someone to work off of. Still, some pairings don't work too well. For example, it's not customary for two sprinters to team up in a combine unless one is a pure pack sprinter and the other is a breakaway sprinter.

I once formed a combine with two friends, Tom and Derek, at a race in Wisconsin. I thought it was obvious that I was the better sprinter of our triumvirate, so when the prime bell rang for a $50 gift certificate, I looked around for my combine-mates. I was expecting a lead-out. Instead, Tom, who obviously thought he was the better sprinter, flew past me and won the first prime handily. From that point on, I settled into the role of trusted domestique and made sure Tom was protected for the rest of the race. You'll come to realize—especially when you're passed by someone going 5 mph faster than you—that you may not be the designated sprinter despite believing that you can sprint.

(Immediately after the race, I did what any self-respecting roadie would do. I checked to see if my brake pads were rubbing on my rim. Alas, they were not.)

A DIFFERENT KIND OF DEAL

Sometimes special deals are worked out between opponents while the racing lamp is lit. As an announcer, I saw it many times: The crowd favorite magically wins the race because he or she struck a deal on the back side of the course away from the adoring crowd. This usually happens in a two-person breakaway in a race that is either in one rider's hometown or in front of one rider's family. But other deals are possible.

At the 1990 Blue Ash Dash criterium in suburban Cincinnati, a miss-and-out race came down to three women who were also friends. Two were from out of state. The third was from Cincinnati. The last lap took an awfully long time, which isn't unheard-of in a miss and out. It can become a game of cat-and-mouse when it's a three-person sprint. In this case, though, things slowed down because one rider was convincing the other two to let her win. The rider from Cincinnati succeeded and came out of the final turn to win a sprint that was worthy of a Tony award.

Surely she paid dearly in cash. Winning carries a price.

Years ago, a friend of mine was in a two-man breakaway and asked his opponent if he could have the win. It would be the first of his career, he cajoled. The opponent let him win.

My friend's coach, Clair Young, who had mentored world champions and Olympic team members, found him after the race and proudly said, "Well, it looks like you finally learned how to win a race!"

My friend nodded and smiled.

"You talked him into letting you win, huh?" said an insightful Clair.

My friend nodded and smiled.

Hey, if you can't win a race with your legs, you may as well try to negotiate.

SHARING THE BOOTY

The real test of character comes at the end of the race, when it is time to share your winnings. You fought hard for that prime. Your combine-mate worked hard to get off the front. You worked very hard to preserve the gap so that he could place in the top five. You managed to sprint for the final paying spot. Awesome. Now, who gets what?

There's no formula for this. It's all negotiated on the spot. Until this moment, the assumption may have been that the split would be even. But now that the money is in your hand, how do you divide it?

That's up to you. And just as in real life, there will be money-grubbers who try to capture every penny they can, and there will be people who don't really care to split hairs. This is hard to see in advance when you're making the arrangement. It's easy to see afterward.

I've seen arguments over this issue. I've seen casual friends become mortal enemies. I know riders who won't speak to each other because of a parking-lot dispute.

My tip for this situation: Race for the love of the sport. You'll rarely be short-changed.

How important was it to you to find someone to work with? And for what reason? Were you motivated by money or the need to actually do something in the race?

That's an important point. We don't simply want to ride in a fast group; we want to play chess at speed. We don't just want to be pack fodder; we want to play the game of bike racing beyond what a solo rider can do.

That's why the combine exists. It's hard to play chess with just one chess piece.

GOING SOLO

Having gone into some detail about the combine, I must also point out the possibilities that exist as a solo rider without teammates. If you know all that's going on between the different teams and teammates within the peloton, you can play off it. If you know who the strong riders are, know their tendencies, know how they race on certain courses, and can identify these things on the fly, then you can put yourself in a position to capitalize on their tactics.

For instance, if two riders from two large teams attack, then you know that their teammates will combine to form a great blocking force at the front of the field. If you're in the right position, you should go with them. You'll have two teams working for you.

Another instance: In the final sprint, if you know that the green team will be lining up in a lead-out train for their sprinter, then you should position yourself behind their sprinter. He will be at or near the end of their lead-out train.

You might also benefit in other ways. I've seen many instances in which a solo rider has ridden away with the race simply because the bigger teams couldn't agree on who should initiate the chase.

"We're not going to chase him. You chase him."

"Well, we're not going to chase him. You chase him."

"Oh, no, that's not our job."

"Oh, yes, it is."

"Oh, no, it's not."

Now, they're not actually saying this out loud, but those are the basic sentiments. And while this is going on, the solo rider is zipping up his jersey in preparation for the photos that will be taken as he crosses the line alone.

Yes, this should remind you of Joop.

8

TIME TRIALS

YOU MIGHT THINK THERE'S LITTLE TO SAY about race tactics in a race that consists of one rider racing against a clock. Granted, strategy isn't a major component, but there are a few tactics that can help you turn in a better time. There's more to it than simply getting the bike out of the car, getting a good warm-up, dialing up your watts, and going fast.

KNOW THE COURSE—INTIMATELY

The first and most obvious tactic required in a time trial is to know the course inside and out (Figure 8.1). Knowing the course will let you know how fast you can take each corner. You'll have no surprises waiting around the next curve. You'll know where to hammer and where to recover.

Ideally, you should ride the course in advance on your time trial bike. If it's a race of great importance, you might ride it more than once. Once slow. Once fast. If you're obsessive about things, you might ride it several times until you have it memorized. The idea is to find the most efficient line through each curve and bend in order to shorten the distance as much as possible.

Many time trial courses that you'll face will be out-and-back races held on a single road with a 180-degree turnaround at the halfway point. The ability

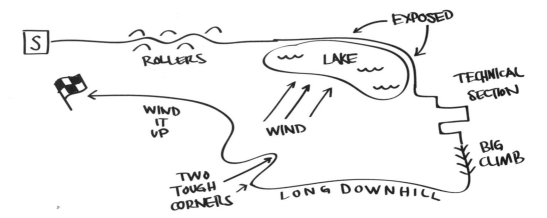

FIGURE 8.1 Make a sketch of your time trial course in advance.

to make this abrupt direction change without scrubbing off all your speed and without crashing is a critical skill. Opinions differ on how best to get through this turn. You should experiment in advance on a similar U-turn until you find which line works best for you.

And now that you're deciding where that perfect line is, I'm about to throw a wrench into the works.

ALL WIND IS NOT CREATED EQUAL

When we ride in a group, we make adjustments for the wind by finding the draft behind the rider in front of us. When we ride a time trial, we usually just accept the wind as a constant that we must battle. Even as the wind shifts, gusts, and swirls, we continue to race using our aero position as our only means of fighting the wind, and we stick to the shortest line through the corners.

Serious time trial specialists spend a large amount of time and energy tweaking their riding position until they've become as aerodynamic as a bullet. Bike manufacturers, too, have spent huge amounts of time and money developing frames that cut through the wind. It's no secret that a watt saved here or there will add up to a faster ride. Wind-tunnel tests, video analysis, and coaching sessions help riders sharpen their riding positions.

But wind is a funny thing.

Wind is not as constant a force as we might imagine. The general direction of the wind may be steady, but the power of the wind can vary greatly. The best way to understand how wind behaves, on a very basic level, is to watch it play across the surface of a lake. It generally doesn't move as one continuous force blowing a steady pattern of ripples; it moves with varying strength. Sometimes the ripples are lined up in ribbons. Sometimes the ripples are over here. Sometimes they're over there. And as we move closer to shore, the trees, houses, and landforms along the shoreline affect the flow of wind.

If we know this, and we know how wind bounces and reflects off surfaces, then we can predict how it will travel down a road. In other words, we can find pockets of calmer air on a windy day by understanding how wind reacts to the ground features, vegetation, and buildings.

> If we are aware of the way that wind bounces and reflects off surfaces, then we can predict how it will travel down a road.

Let me paint a picture as a starting point. If you're riding on a road through open farmland, the wind will be fairly direct. That is, with nothing to interrupt its flow, the wind will generally have a steady force and direction. But let's say you're riding down a straight road that is lined with pine trees on the left side. A strong wind is coming from your two o'clock. (For those of you who wear digital watches, it's coming at an angle from the right.)

Where is that wind going to be the strongest?

The wind might be reflecting off the pine trees. It might also be slowed by the pine trees, creating a pocket of still air near the trees. It might be channeling itself along the trees, creating a stronger wall of wind near the trees. It might be whipping over the trees, creating a swirling tailwind in your direction.

Now let's add a row of trees to the right side of the road so that we're riding through a trench of sorts created by the trees. (Imagine the Death Star trench scene in *Star Wars*.) If the wind is still coming from two o'clock, the strongest jet of air will now be in a completely different location. Depending on the strength, height of the trees, and angle of the wind, it could do any number of things. And as we wind our way along the course, everything that is near the road—trees, barricades, tanning salons, gas stations, parked cars—will play with the wind.

Similarly, watch how a river flows. The substrate and banks of the river create eddies and whirlpools. The current will rarely be constant.

My point is not that we can always predict the exact location of the strongest wind but that we need to explore where that wind might be. And, per the preceding discussion, that the shortest line through a time trial course may not always the fastest line, depending on where the strongest winds are found.

In a race in which seconds count, if I can find a headwind that is 3 mph lower (less forceful) on one side of the road than the other, then it behooves me to find it and ride in it.

Three-time world champion and Olympic gold medalist Chris Boardman said that he looked at everything when he pre-rode a time trial course. Not just the roadway but also everything around it and how it would affect the wind, and how that might affect his race.

Even if you never ride a time trial in your life, a better understanding of wind will only help you in cycling. For example, in your next solo breakaway. On a criterium course in a downtown area, the wind will be whipping through the buildings, and with a little trial and error, you'll probably be able to find the calmer winds.

But if you continue to believe that wind is a steady and constant force that comes down the road like a parade, you're probably wasting energy somewhere on the course.

KNOW YOUR OPPONENT

Obviously, your main opponent in the time trial is your pesky alter ego who is constantly reminding you, "This hurts." Block that opponent out.

Other opponents include the weather and the course. But the other riders whom you'll share the course with will also factor in to your race.

If you know that the two riders in front of you are stronger or weaker than you, then you should be able to gauge your relative effort according to what they're doing. If you can normally beat your minute man (the rider who starts 1 minute before you), how long should it take you to catch him? If he's someone you can beat with one leg tied behind your back, then you should be worried if he's pulling away from you.

(In fact, if you can ride with one leg tied behind your back, you should join the circus.)

When I was a naive and mediocre Cat. IV racer, I entered a small stage race that started with a time trial. I didn't realize that I was the last Cat. IV rider to start, nor did I realize that the first Cat. III rider starting 1 minute behind me was a local legend. So when he passed me, I knew enough not to draft off him, but I did my best to keep him in my sights because I assumed (incorrectly) that he and I were equals. I struggled badly but managed to finish just a few hundred yards behind him and unwittingly rode into the top placing in my category because I was too stupid to figure out that I was going much faster than I had ever gone. Had I known he was a former state champion, I probably would have been psyched out and thus left behind. Today I would make a conscious effort to do what I did then: use him as a guidepost during my ride.

(For the record, I am still a mediocre racer, but I am no longer naive.)

Pay attention to who else is in the queue as you await your start. Know their strengths. They will provide feedback that your power meter and heart rate monitor will miss.

Chris Horner   TOUR TTT WITH KLODI

Prior to the 2011 Tour de France, our RadioShack team spent several days training together to prepare for the critical team time trial (TTT) that we would face on stage 2. Klodi—our teammate Andreas Klöden—was time trialing like a madman that particular year, and before the Tour he was smashing the team to bits during training days.

I was the not-so-lucky first guy behind him in the team rotation during training, and I was absolutely destroyed every single day trying not only to hold on to his wheel but also to pull through after he had finished his time on the front and then rotated off. After the last training ride, while we were on the team bus, I argued to the team that Klodi needed to slow his pace down in order to keep the team together. It was easy to predict that whichever rider was next to pull after Klodi (who at the moment was going to be me) had no chance of finishing the race with the team.

My voice went unheard, however; everyone else thought it was absolutely necessary for Klodi to continue riding at the same pace during the

→

CLIMBING AND DESCENDING IN A TT

While the common wisdom about the time trial is to hammer through it at your power threshold the whole time, there are places on almost every time trial course where it's smart to chill.

A climb is a great place to cook yourself, often to bad effect. As you hammer yourself into the ground on an uphill section, ask yourself this: How much time am I gaining by killing myself on this climb? And would I be smarter to ride tempo up the climb and make up time on other parts of the course? Or

TOUR TTT WITH KLODI, CONTINUED

race in order for the team to have a chance at winning the stage. I could easily see that I wasn't going to win the argument, so it was time for my backup plan: at least save myself and rotate positions so I could get as far away from Klodi as possible. After I had begged for a different position, Dmitri Muravyev, our Kazakh teammate, stood up in the bus and offered to take my spot.

When race day arrived, Dmitri lasted all of about four rotations before he was no longer able to stay with the team. When we had finally crossed the finish line and made it back to the bus, had showered, and were on our way home, Dmitri was still so upset about getting dropped that I felt the need to reassure him that no one on the team could have possibly survived behind that particular wheel. On that day, unfortunately, my predictions were correct, but because I could see it coming, I lived to fight another day. ◾

should I just bury myself in a hole of pain that will take several kilometers from which to recover?

Downhill sections are a great place to go really fast, but if pedaling only gains you a few miles per hour and therefore a few measly seconds, you might be better off soft-pedaling on the way down. Sure, there are gradients that can be helped by pedaling, but some should be viewed as an opportunity to take a break, sip some water, and allow your heart rate to come down a little.

Being familiar with the course will allow you to plan out these areas. For instance, if you know that a long descent is coming up in the next mile, you can afford to push a little harder knowing that you'll soon have the ability to recover.

MAN AND MACHINE

Though you may have gone to great lengths to refine your aerodynamic position using a wind tunnel and computer diagnostics—or perhaps an oscillating fan and a friend with a video camera—the truth is that a time trial requires a few different positions on the bike. You may think that the tightest, lowest aerodynamic position is the one you'll use most, but can you really ride like that for the entire race?

Pro riders have a couple of different positions on their time trial bikes. They have the upright position in which they are at their least aerodynamic. They have their super-aero position that can cut through steel. And they also have something in between that is a cross between comfort and efficiency.

The upright position is used to negotiate tight corners and tricky parts of the course. The aero position is used for the places where the highest speeds are attained and where the strongest headwind is felt. The in-between position is used for the rest of the ride. It's fast and efficient, but it's not going to tax the body more than what needs to be done to make the bike go fast.

Most riders worry too much about their aerodynamic position on the time trial bike without realizing that the body needs to be comfortable in order to create the power necessary to make the bike go fast. The road is not a perfect scientific model. What's more important is concentration, breathing, and a lack of tension in nonessential muscles. Aerodynamics are but a small piece of the pie.

9

HIGH ALERT

BIKE RACING IS KIND OF LIKE A SCARY MOVIE; you can almost predict when something is going to jump out at you and make your heart race. In the movie, it's when the camera is moving slowly down a dimly lit hallway, passing open doors leading to darkened spaces. Nothing is moving. The violins are sustaining a note that is uncomfortably high. The lead character is the last remaining cast member still in possession of her head. The others have all been lopped off by a hatchet-wielding escapee from the asylum.

Yeah, that's almost exactly like bike racing. The similarities are astounding. Something is about to happen, and it ain't pretty.

In a bike race, there are moments when you need to be on high alert because the tone of the race can change drastically and quickly. These are moments that catch some people off guard. Those people usually get dropped.

Unfortunately, there is no musical score to tip you off to the impending shift; you have to sing that part yourself. Quietly.

Here are a few of the elements that can quickly turn a race into a riot, especially if you do it right.

HEAVY WIND

Wind isn't usually sudden, and it rarely sneaks up on you. When you step out of the car and your USAC participant release form flies across the parking lot, you'll know that there's wind present.

Yet what surprises many riders is how much harder a bike race is on a windy day. On a calm day, most of the headwind is created by the pack's speed. But on a windy day, the effect is multiplied. The draft behind a rider is smaller. Gaps grow bigger faster. Closing a gap is harder. As riders struggle to find the draft, side-to-side motion is amplified, causing more crashes. Yes, wind has a nasty effect on a peloton.

On a windy day, you need to be on high alert for gaps opening in front of you. Riders who are struggling need only falter a little bit before they find themselves losing ground quickly. As they lose ground, a gap opens. As soon as it does, the alarm bells should start ringing for everyone behind the struggling riders. Don't hesitate, and don't expect them to close the gap themselves. They won't. Go around and close the gap as quickly as possible.

To do this, you need to be aware of what's happening in front of the rider in front of you, which is difficult when you're tucking in to avoid the headwind. Don't fall asleep back there and assume that everyone else is keeping pace.

If the gap grows and becomes an outright split in the field, you have a decision to make: Bite the bullet and jump across the gap while it's small, or hope that everyone works together to bring the field back together. I'll warn you now, the former is preferred. The latter is risky.

As the field falls apart into several smaller groups, keep track of the power riders. If you're in the third group surrounded by all of the strong guys, don't panic. They'll bring it back together. If you're in the third group surrounded by bird watchers, panic.

Whenever you're fighting a heavy wind, it helps to find a rider bigger than you to draft off. Be aware of who is in front of you when the pace picks up or when the race turns into the windy section of the course. Don't wait until things get strung out to discover that you're stuck behind Stuart Little. Instead, look for someone like Sulley, the big bear-shaped creature from *Monsters, Inc.*

And if you find that everyone is fighting to be on your wheel when you're headed into the wind, then it should be apparent to you that you are Sulley.

CAUGHT

You were in a breakaway. You were working to stay away from the pack. You had been rotating your little paceline for several laps, enjoying the freedom from the peloton. You had a decent gap at one point, but now you're caught.

Now what?

Be on high alert.

Whenever a breakaway gets caught, whether you were in it or not, some riders will expect a moment of inactivity, as if they might get a moment to relax and think about their next move or admire the result of their chase effort. That's an unreasonable expectation. Instead, this is the moment when another attack will likely launch off the front. The field will be tired from the chase effort that caught the breakaway, so anyone who has fresh legs will seize this opportunity to attack.

Know this in advance. Be ready.

WHEN A CRASH OCCURS

What do you do when a crash occurs?

First, be on high alert for another crash to happen as a result. Some riders will turn to see the first crash, which will cause them to run into someone. Some will hit the brakes. Keep your eyes forward and be ready for anything.

If a crash occurs behind you, your first instinct may be to attack. This raises a moral question. Is it OK? Is it unsportsmanlike? Is it wrong to benefit from someone else's misfortune? Or is that just bike racing?

Believe it or not, there are widely varying opinions in this debate.

The fact is, all of those opinions are present in your race, and you'll need to respond to the ones who believe it's OK to attack. They will accelerate immediately at the first sound of a crash. And they will accelerate hard. Be ready for it.

Maybe I should rephrase that: At the first sound of a crash, make sure that you're not going to be involved in the crash. Once that's settled, be ready for the hard acceleration.

Yeah, that's what I meant.

If you're caught behind a crash, you need to quickly jump into chase mode. And don't lollygag. Seconds count as you pick your way through the rubble. The front half of the peloton likely accelerated at the sound of skidding rubber and crunching carbon fiber. They are putting distance on everyone else at a fast rate. For example, if the front group is riding at 25 mph, every second that you hesitate lengthens the gap by another 38 feet.

> *If you're caught behind a crash, you need to quickly jump into chase mode.*

Pro riders are trained to look out for their team leader. If he hits the deck, they will need to help him get back up and rolling. You will also see them react a little more nonchalantly than we do in the amateur ranks. This is because they will likely have the benefit of the caravan vehicles to help tow them back up to the lead group.

Amateur riders with the presence of mind to look around when a crash takes riders down will look for their teammates in this moment of crisis and help each other back into the fray, but they will do so in a bigger hurry.

Either way, if you find yourself delayed because of a crash, look around for teammates or stronger riders who are also delayed. They'll be chasing to get back in the race, and you can work together with them. There's no need to chase all by yourself.

CLOUDBURST

We already know the different ways that riders react to rain, so we shouldn't be taken by surprise when it actually happens. We should anticipate it.

I was in a race recently in which nothing was getting away from the clutches of the peloton. It had rained earlier in the race, but the roads had dried. Many attacks had tried to escape, but none had succeeded. With about 10 miles of racing remaining, we were a tightly bunched pack of soon-to-be sprinters hurtling toward the finish line. As I was looking for any way to avoid that mad dash to the line against 70 other riders, I found myself looking skyward.

I was hoping for a cloudburst.

I understand how futile it is to hope for the weather to change in order to effect change in a race, but that was about the only thing that would have broken this race up.

When a sudden cloudburst strikes a race, it usually creates an amazing level of panic among the riders. All of the riders who hate riding in the rain usually stop pedaling, and all of those who love the rain usually drop the hammer. Wherever you fall in the continuum between those two extremes will determine whether the pack splits behind you or in front of you. Be ready for drama.

APPROACHING ARENBERG FOREST

Every now and then, a racecourse will feature a particularly tough section. Perhaps it's a mile of gravel road. Maybe it's a very narrow roadway. Or it could be a hill known to locals as "the wall." If you live in a mountainous region, hills may not faze you one bit. But it only takes one big hill to strike fear into the hearts of flatlanders in the peloton.

You've seen Paris–Roubaix enough times to know how the peloton approaches the stretch of cobbles in the Arenberg Forest. You should imagine the same reaction in your race, and know the pace is going to go ballistic once you hit the famous whatever it is—wall, gravel, narrow section, whatever. You also should know that all the other riders have read this book and know that they have to get themselves to the front. Therefore, expect the pace to begin ramping up long before the climb/gravel/narrow section begins. Don't be caught napping in the back of the pack.

FIRST FIVE LAPS, LAST FIVE LAPS

As obvious as this point may be, it still deserves emphasis: The first five laps and the last five laps of a criterium are especially dynamic. The same holds true for the last kilometers of a road race. This is not to diminish what's happening in the middle part of the race, but the beginning and the end are particularly challenging. In the beginning of the race, riders are trying to get to the front to join the attacks. At the end of the race, riders are trying to get in position to win.

Seldom does the first breakaway of the day succeed. In fact, most riders will tell you that it never succeeds. They are wrong. It happens. For example, Jens Voigt rode away in the first 5 miles of stage 4 of the 2012 USA Pro Challenge and rode the entire 97 miles from Aspen to Beaver Creek solo. In the 1993 Superweek, 10 riders opened up a gap within the first half mile of the Road America stage. The pack never saw them again.

Successful first breaks do happen, and you have to pay attention.

Be alert at both ends. If something happens at the beginning of the race, you'll still have time to recover. But if something dramatic happens in the closing laps or miles, it may be too late to react.

Of course, one thing to look for in the final laps of a race is the sudden appearance of all the riders who have been sitting at the back of the pack for the entire race. They've been waiting for this moment to move forward and get active. You forgot about them because you hadn't heard from them since the start of the race. Don't be surprised by this influx of fresh legs. They probably did the same thing last week, too.

Another thing to watch for in the closing laps of a race is riders who have reached their limit and start to fade. Actually, "start to fade" may be overly polite. In reality, they've blown up. They're dropping like a rock. If you're not on the ball, they may sweep you out of the race. Keep your eyes open for deadwood going backward.

If you get gapped off the back by a dropping rider, you have the opportunity to yell at him and call him names, but it would be better for you to use that energy to sprint around him and stay in contact with the lead group.

Your choice.

WHEN TO RELAX

Just as there are moments during a race when you should be on high alert, there are also moments when it's OK to relax.

There are times in a race when no one is racing. This is known as "the calm before the storm." Collectively, the entire group will sit up and take it easy for a while. It's one of those moments in sport in which everyone is ready for nothing to happen. (In baseball, this is known as "the entire game.")

It's not a crime for a race to go slowly. Some people let it drive them crazy, as if all races are supposed to go supersonic from start to finish. But look: We know that the race is going to have a high average speed when all is said and done. Getting to that average speed might mean a lull riding at 15 mph to counterbalance the torrid pace that comes later. When that lull happens, you must force yourself into rest mode. Take advantage of every easy pedal stroke. Drink. Breathe. Stretch. Save your energy for when the race explodes. And whatever you do, do not attack.

If you attack when things are going slowly, you're attacking when everyone is rested. Sure, you may get a big gap in a short amount of time, but since everyone has recovered, they'll have no trouble ramping up the speed and catching you.

After a lull runs its course, things will pick up again. Wait for it. The average speed must be reached, after all.

In my region, the Cat. I/II races average somewhere in the neighborhood of 27 mph. No matter how fast or slow we seem to go, I find that the average is always in that neighborhood when I check my computer at the end of the race.

(Actually, that average speed takes into account the first mile of cooldown riding after the finish line because I always forget to stop my timer when I cross the line.)

Stage 3 of the 2009 Tour of California traveled down the coast from San Francisco to Santa Cruz. Once the breakaway was safely off the front of the field, the peloton crawled along at 16 mph. You could have ridden a beach cruiser and stayed with them. Meanwhile, the breakaway jumped out to a 15-minute lead.

The average speed for that day was 26 mph. To reach that average after riding at 16 mph for 3 hours, the pack had to break the sound barrier.

WHEN RACES GO WRONG

Bike racing is normally a full-on, nonstop race to the finish while adhering to the rules as closely as possible, but there are times when a form of democracy develops in a bike race. It's a majority-rule, self-policing, all-for-one/one-for-all phenomenon that crops up at odd times.

Take, for example, the 1992 Athens Brick Criterium in Athens, Ohio.

A crash toward the tail end of the race caused a neutralization followed by a lengthy delay. When the crash occurred, there was a 9-man breakaway with a 3-man chase group located in the middle of a 20-second gap.

After the neutralization, the officials restarted the race as one group. They felt that the gaps had not been fully established at the time of the crash, so they didn't attempt to re-create the breakaways. The peloton felt otherwise. Within two laps of the restart, the dissatisfied peloton rolled to a stop at the finish line and asked to be restarted with the gaps restored. The officials complied.

A few laps later, the race looked just as it had before the crash. Experienced racers have the uncanny ability to keep track of who is where and by what margin.

By the very nature of the sport, it is almost impossible for the officiating crew to see the entire race. At large events they will use motorcycle officials to monitor the happenings within the peloton, but at smaller events you'll be lucky to have one official in a following car. Still, safety and fairness are important to each race, so it then falls upon the riders to self-police and often make decisions to preserve order and safety within the group.

For instance, in a road race with several fields on the course at once, it's possible that one field may catch and overtake another. The rules state that the slower field shall yield to the overtaking field. That is, those riders must temporarily neutralize their race and move to the right to allow the overtaking field to safely pass. Invariably, however, one rider in the slower field will see this as an opportunity to attack and get lost in the faster field, thus hoping to sneak away to the finish.

Don't be that rider.

Everyone else in the race will be on to you, and they will not look fondly upon your move. You will develop a reputation that will stick with you for years.

Conversely, if you are in the faster field, you are certainly permitted to attack as you approach a slower field from behind. You can treat the slower field as an obstacle for your chasers to deal with. That's a smart move that doesn't paint you in a bad light. In fact, you probably won't be the only one to think of it.

Other examples of democracy on wheels that I've seen with my own eyes include:

- An entire peloton missing a turn and riding 2 miles off course. The group stopped, turned around, and waited for some riders to urinate before resuming the race.

- An entire peloton sprinting for the finish line only to come face-to-face with a pile of bikes and bodies and general carnage from the previous field's sprint that hadn't ended so well. The sprinting riders hit the brakes and came to an abrupt stop. The chief referee gave them three options: They could ride another lap; they could ride the final kilometer again; they could all debate the finishing order among themselves. Believe it or not, they chose the third option and sorted everything out on paper based on what had been happening at the time they were neutralized. No one complained.

- The peloton taking a wrong turn on the course and ending up in front of the breakaway. It was an accident, I swear! How was I to know where that road led?

- In a combined field of masters 45+ and 55+ male riders, a group of 10 masters 45+ riders breaking away and staying away. It was obvious they would never be seen again. Their race paid only to 8 places. In cycling terms, "All the money had gone up the road." During the last 5 miles of the race, the remaining 45+ riders dropped to the back of the pack and allowed the 55+ riders to race unhindered at the front of the field.

- A masters 35+ field catching a Cat. III field, causing a game of leapfrog that lasted for 15 miles as speeds fluctuated between the two fields. It became a tangled mess that was also quite dangerous; each time they passed each other, they took up the entire width of the road. Eventually the Cat. IIIs collectively decided to stop and allow the masters to move ahead to a safe interval before resuming their race.

Chris Horner   SOMETIMES YOU GOTTA REGROUP

Shortly after the start of a stage in a race in Switzerland several years ago—I don't remember whether it was the Tour de Suisse or the Tour of Romandie—hail the size of golf balls started pummeling the race. Now, I know everyone says that the hail they saw was the size of golf balls, but this time the hail actually was the size of golf balls. A break of riders had just started to form off the front of the field, and the main group was beginning to shatter into numerous smaller bunches under the stress of the attacks. Then the hail hit.

Everyone immediately jumped off their bikes and ran into the forest alongside the road for cover. I was huddled next to Thomas Löfkvist; we squished up against the side of the mountain while holding his rain jacket over our heads as a cover from the bombardment.

When the hail finally stopped, my hand that had been holding the jacket was bruised around the knuckles from the hail hitting it so hard, and the road that we had been racing on was completely covered in white. It looked like the aftermath of a zombie apocalypse, with $12,000 race bikes abandoned all over the road, ditches, and forest. The spare bikes on top of the team cars had holes and cracks through the carbon top tubes from being hit by the hail, and the cars themselves were a mass of broken windshields and dented metal.

Before the race resumed, the riders agreed that we would all restart as one large group, even though the field had clearly been blowing apart into smaller groups—including an established break—prior to the storm. On that day, survival was more important than whatever was happening in the race. ◾

- A dog on the course.
- A car on the course.
- A dog driving a car on the course.

Whether or not you agree with the decision of the pack, the majority rules, and it usually makes the right decision during strange circumstances. The key to handling an unexpected situation is communication. Be vocal about unexpected threats. Don't be shy in directing the field to stop and reboot. Speak up about infractions that threaten the safety of the group or the fairness of the outcome. And never attempt to capitalize on circumstances that are far outside bike racing. For instance, never attempt to catch a draft from the lead vehicle if it drifts too close to the front of the field it's leading. Never try to gain a competitive advantage from a poorly timed alien invasion. If Martians attack during your race, you have much bigger things to worry about than, say, placing fifth.

If Martians attack during your race, would you even notice? I mean, you probably didn't notice the dog driving the car.

SUFFERING, TAILGUNNING, PUNCHING TICKETS

If I've made it sound as though I'm a top-level elite racer, I apologize. Nothing could be further from the truth. On a good day, I may make it to the front once—when everyone else stops to pee. But I am proud to call myself field fodder in the best possible way. I'm safe. I'm capable. I have mad skills and a high threshold for pain. I know enough to stay out of the way. And I also take pride in being able to sit in with just about any caliber amateur field.

If I've ever exchanged words with riders in a breakaway, it was when they lapped the field and made contact with the back of the pack where I was riding.

I will ask that you give a little extra respect to those riders, like me, at the back of the pack who choose to suffer. It isn't as easy as it looks. It is, in fact, an art form.

As I said at the beginning of this book, not everyone is in the race to win it. Some are just there for the atmosphere and the burning legs.

Riders will gladly struggle through a 90-minute race if only to see the finish line. We show up at races with less-than-perfect fitness, and we sit on the back of the pack with our tongues hanging out because the pain we feel on the road is much less than the pain we feel on the curb. It's more painful to watch our friends race without us.

It's the addiction that we all share of being in that vortex of sight and sound. To hear the freewheels chatter. To hear the chains grind. Whether we're fully prepared for it or not.

And let's not pretend that this only happens at the amateur level with riders dangling at the bottoms of their respective categories. It happens at the professional levels, usually in January and February, with riders who are struggling to regain fitness. It's all relative, of course, but they struggle with the same temptations in the off-season as we amateurs do: sweets, drinks, television, and so on. And when the racing season arrives a little too soon, they are living as we do: struggling to hang on.

So I would like to take a few moments to discuss some of the tactics that these riders develop. Yes, it's OK to call them survival techniques.

Pay attention. You may need to use them someday.

Front or Back?

For someone who is not in great race shape, is it easier to survive a bike race by riding near the front of the pack or the back? Tough call.

For the rider who stays near the front of the pack, the pace up there is usually pretty steady provided he or she just sits in and doesn't try to respond to the attacks. That can make the front a good place to hang out for someone who is not in good shape. But accelerations are hard on the weak and frail. I know for a fact.

Chris Horner   TOUR DE FRANCE SURVIVAL

At one point in the 2006 Tour de France, I had become very ill and was fighting just to make it to the finish line with the gruppetto (the last group still in the race). On this particular day, I had already been sick for two days and suffering very badly. By the third stage, I had had just about all I could take when we hit a category 4 climb. Normally I could have passed over the top of this climb in the front group without any problems whatsoever, but that was not the case on this day. Before we were even a few pedal strokes into the climb, I was already coming unglued and going backward through the field, but this is another instance where experience and age definitely paid off.

First, I called up the team car and had them pass me two fresh water bottles, with a little bit of acceleration from the car as I grabbed each of the bottles, slinging me forward to the back of the field. This helped me for a little bit, though soon I could not stay with the field any longer.

But I had crashed hard a few stages earlier, and now it was time to take advantage of whatever help my crash injuries could bring me during this crisis stage. I raised my hand again and called for the medical car.

→

For the rider at the back, there's more draft to be found, but there's also more of the accordion effect. If we're racing on a technical criterium course, the change in tempo caused by the many corners will make it very difficult. That's the bad news.

The interesting thing is that by race's end, both riders will have the same average speed. But the rider who stayed near the front will likely have higher peaks.

TOUR DE FRANCE SURVIVAL, CONTINUED

Every good European pro knows that as long as the medical car is servicing you, you have permission to hold on to the car. As soon as the car pulled up, I asked the doctor to spray some numbing spray on my open wounds. After he attended to the wounds—and for the record, I pointed out every single open wound I could find for him—I waited until he had put everything back into his medical bag before I asked him if he could please cover them up with bandages, too.

By the time he had finished covering the open wounds, we were almost to the top of the climb, but not quite there. I needed one last bit of help from the doc before the climb would finish. Once again, I waited until he had put his entire medical bag away before I asked him for some Advil. His expression was priceless, as he once again had to open up his bag and unload all of the contents he had just put away in order to reach the Advil, which was of course at the bottom of the bag. He handed me a couple of tablets just as the climb was finishing. I thanked him, took a big sling off the side mirror of the car, and rejoined the back of the group just as the climb finished. ◾

Helping a Brother Out

Riders who are struggling to hang on to the back of the pack are a considerate lot. We are always on the lookout for riders who have popped, and we will warn each other of possible challenges. For instance, we'll point out falling deadwood.

"Heads up."

"He's cooked. Go around him."

This warning prevents our compatriot from being swept out of the group.

We will also give warnings to a rider who is dropping back to recover from a hard effort at the front. These are riders who have expended themselves at the front, are dropping fast, and are looking for the back of the train. They're waiting until the last possible second to accelerate, thus milking every available second of recovery before accelerating up to speed again to hop onto the caboose.

Sometimes they drop so fast that they are unaware that they've reached the back of the pack so quickly. This is probably due to the fact that the pack is much smaller than it was at the start of the race.

"Geez, where'd everybody go?" one will ask, not realizing that it was probably his pacesetting that cooked off half of the field. As he drops, we'll give him a verbal warning that the end of the line is coming.

"Up up."

"This is it," we usually say.

Almost every time, they thank us. And we feel as if we've done a good deed. It's not that we're trying to help them, necessarily. Our motivations are quite selfish. We're trying to preserve more riders in front of us to help block the wind. If they get dropped, that's one less wheel to suck.

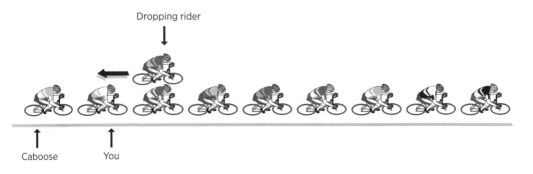

FIGURE 9.1 Hopping onto the caboose: You can choose how nice you want to be depending on how much warning you give to the dropping rider.

I've been in that position before, believe it or not. I was off the front in a breakaway that was going much faster than I had ever experienced. I was in over my head, and I knew it. I was thankful when we were caught. I was cooked. And as I dropped back through the field, I looked over my shoulder, hoping to find the absolute back of the pack. I would need to time my effort so that I could hop onto the back as it flew by me. Were it not for the warning that a rider gave me, I surely would have missed the caboose and gotten dropped from the race.

"Up, Smith. Up!"

Good deed, my friend. Good deed.

"Where were you?" they asked. They hadn't seen me for several laps, so they assumed I had dropped out.

"I was in the breakaway," I said proudly.

"Right," they replied flatly.

"Seriously. I was."

"Yeah, whatever."

Rather than argue, I simply returned to my routine of calculating my chances of finishing the race.

Struggling riders can always tell you the exact number of laps remaining. We are wizards at gauging our output to give the absolute minimum effort necessary in order to live to see the number 1 on the lap cards and to hear the sweet ringing of the bell. We never lose track of the lap count.

If we pop during an extended hammer session and get dropped from the race, it is a universal law that the field will sit up, drink, chat, and freewheel along at 18 mph just moments after we officially retire.

Happens. Every. Single. Time.

DNF Versus Finish at All Costs

Roadies will debate at length whether it is better to finish the race at all costs or withdraw from the race when you're no longer in contention. Pick your poison.

If your legs need the extra miles that come with completing the course, go for it.

If you would rather not get the extra attention that comes with being the last finisher, then you may want to slink back to your car unnoticed.

On a criterium course, I recommend making a quiet disappearance on the back side of the course. Stay out of the way of the race. Don't become a traffic cone that they have to dodge. Yes, you are entitled to remain in the race until the officials ask you to retire, but in reality you are more of a hazard than a competitor at this point.

On a road racecourse, you must follow the rules of the road once you fall out of the race envelope. If the official follow vehicles have passed you, you are considered a bicycle pedestrian by most state laws. Ride safely back to your car and live to ride another day.

Please do not roll across the finish line two hours after the podium ceremony expecting the timing equipment to capture your finish.

It's a bitter pill to swallow when you get dropped from a bike race. But depending on your level of fatigue, getting home safely should be your first priority. Don't make them scramble the rescue helicopters to look for you.

10

ASSEMBLING THE PERFECT TEAM

RECREATIONAL CYCLING IS A CLUB-BASED ACTIVITY. Bike racing is a team-based sport. Clubs and teams can form in various ways. Therefore, the path to becoming a racing team member isn't the same for everyone, and the dynamics of the teams will vary.

According to USAC, there were 2,812 registered cycling clubs in the United States in 2012. These clubs offer a multitude of bike racing experiences, from touring to BMX racing to track cycling and everything in between. Many of these cycling clubs contain a road racing faction.

Some clubs are created only for road racing and offer no other type of racing or riding to their members. These teams might actively recruit new members and may have strict bylaws that govern their riders, requiring them to attend a given number of races per year, for instance, or to wear the team kit at all times on the bike. If the members participate in tours or charity rides, they'll do so as much for the training miles as for the fellowship that these rides offer. (They'll be encouraged to wear a disguise and register using a pseudonym.)

Most clubs have an open-door policy, meaning anyone with a heartbeat is welcome to join. They may have membership drives in order to invite new members. These clubs are welcoming of all and therefore have a wide variety of styles and abilities. A bike racing team that forms within such a club will also have riders with a wide range of abilities.

Some teams actively recruit new riders, actually targeting specific riders from other clubs in order to bolster their racing roster. They will offer free equipment, paid travel, or paid entry fees in an effort to attract better riders. This approach may cause some hard feelings within the local racing community. No team enjoys having its stars lured away to other teams. Rider poaching is done more aggressively in some parts of the country than in others.

Other clubs won't recruit, nor will they welcome new riders. Those clubs will likely disband in a few years due to a lack of member interest. When the last remaining member of a club dies, that'll probably be the end of it.

As we focus on the team aspect of the sport, there are some things to look for when selecting a club or a team:

- Does the club have a specific racing program? Or does it just have a few members who race?
- Does the team have a designated coach? Or is there no defined leader?
- Does the team travel to each race together as a group? Or do the riders just show up and see who else is there?
- Is the team's sole objective to win races, or is it OK simply to have fun and do your best?
- Do the team members train together regularly? Or do they train individually?

What's important to you? If you're an up-and-coming young prospect with aspirations of making it to the pro ranks, you should be looking for a serious team with a dedicated coach. If you're a casual racer who enjoys the camaraderie of the sport, you may only need a club setting with some racers of a similar mind-set.

Or you can pick the one with the coolest jersey. That works, too.

Many riders base their selection on the team or club that gives its riders the most free stuff. This is understandable for riders who may not be able to afford the expense of the sport and must find ways to economize. Ideally, though, you should look for the team that will help you develop your skills to the fullest or the team to which you feel you can contribute the most.

Which type of club will have more success? The biggest club? The richest club? The club with all the fast riders? It's difficult to say. Generally, the club with members who communicate best will enjoy the most success, for those riders will be good at organizing to train, schedule, and race as a team.

RECRUITING

Perhaps you're building a new team from the ground up or just recruiting a few new riders. If so, you must consider many things when sizing up prospective teammates. For example, what role do you envision for them? Are they sprinters, climbers, or all-rounders? Can they sit on the front of the pack and make it go fast for hours? Are they fearless in the final miles?

You also have a bunch of other things to consider. Some simple, some complex.

Do your prospective members have a good work ethic? Do they have a good nutrition program? Do they ride smart? Or are they "strong like bull; smart like tractor"?

Are they dependable? Are they easy to get hold of? Communication is as important off the bike as on the bike. It shouldn't be an ordeal to organize a Sunday ride or distribute team clothing.

Do they live nearby? Will you be able to train with them? Rarely can a team race as a team when its riders are scattered across a region and meet only at the races. To race as a team on Sunday, it helps to ride as a team on Tuesday.

Pro teams can get away with having far-flung members because it's the nature of the beast. They come from far and wide, and they travel far and wide, and it's their job to be familiar with their teammates' abilities. Plus, they're all fairly evenly matched in ability and know-how. It's not as complicated as it is at the amateur level. With the varying abilities in the amateur ranks, there's actually more to become familiar with.

Are your prospective recruits as dedicated as your current teammates? This goes back to the discussion about motivation. Are they racers who want to race a lot? Or are they hobbyists who want to race a little? Are they committed to road racing? Or do they also want to dabble in mountain bike races and an occasional triathlon? Are they just coming into their prime? Or are they on the back end of their career? Just because they have a long list of top finishes doesn't guarantee that they'll still be motivated and committed next season.

I like to tell the story of a team that aggressively recruited a rider by offering free clothing and paid entry fees. The rider was hesitant, so the team upped its offer by adding a new bike. Still the rider hesitated. The team decided to offer travel money and free foot rubs. That sealed the deal.

A month later, the rider was accepted into a master's program at the local university, which left him almost no time to train. The team was angry.

The end.

CHEMISTRY

There's a school of team-building thought that says to forget about strengths and talents. Forget about dependability and loyalty. The most important issue is chemistry.

I happen to agree with this approach. Here's why. Since you'll be traveling, training, and racing together, how you get along off the bike is as important as how you perform on the bike. At some point in your cycling life, you'll meet a rider who has the speed of a cheetah and the lungs of a horse. And he or she will be a complete head case.

What do you do?

The season is long. Bike racing is hard. You don't need to invite more drama and anxiety by adding a high-maintenance diva to the mix. Unless, of course, your diva can win every race and is willing to share all winnings.

Pro riders will tell you what a drain it is to have to deal with someone who makes life difficult in the team bus. The constant attention required to coddle and reassure a high-maintenance teammate can really get in the way of team chemistry. If you're spending too much time worrying about how someone will react to, say, bad service at a restaurant, you're burning matches even before you get to the hotel.

Life on the road is challenging. Traveling with six adults can sometimes be like traveling with six children.

I had a teammate years ago who refused to use rest-area bathrooms. That made road trips a challenge. For him.

Cyclists can be an unsympathetic bunch.

On the other hand, it's possible for a rider to get invited to join a team based solely on his off-bike behavior. I know of one instance in which a rider whose ability was only adequate was brought aboard an elite team simply because he was hilarious and fun to have along on road trips.

No, it wasn't me. But thanks for asking.

SACRIFICE

If you aren't willing to walk through fire for your teammates, you may not be ready for a team sport such as cycling. It's another unique aspect of our sport: The team wins, but one rider gets all the glory. There's room for only one on the podium, which is a shame because we all know that it takes more than one to get

Chris Horner   DIFFICULT TEAMMATES

Difficult teammates exist on just about every team. I'm always surprised when the general cycling fan believes that everyone in bike racing, and especially teammates, is the best of friends. I always respond with the same question: "Does everyone in your office get along?" Clearly, there are always going to be teammates who are great friends, but most are simply work colleagues. And some are even less than that. I've yet to get through a Tour de France where every teammate is on the same page, let along doing what he is supposed to at every moment. I've seen riders protecting their top-20 spot in GC while a teammate in the top 10 was in danger of losing his.

I've also had teammates whom I've liked very much but who have still been very difficult to race with. One particular sprinter on an early team of mine could never make up his mind during the race whether or not he had the legs to sprint for the win. This often left the team in chaos during races, as we would chase down the breakaway even though it had one of our teammates in it, in order to better our team chances for the win with a field sprint. But then our sprinter would tell us that his legs were no good just as we were catching the break—that had our teammate in it already! ◼

there. (The Olympic Committee would do our sport a great favor by awarding team medals in the Olympic road race instead of an individual medal to the winner. Just think of the water-cooler conversations cyclists could have with coworkers confused by the concept of teamwork in a bike race.) Unheralded teammates give up their own chances of winning to make it happen.

That's the ideal. That's how we expect it to work. Sacrifices must be made in order for the team concept to be effective. However, it doesn't always work that way.

Many teams suffer from an unspoken rivalry among riders. On these squads, members become more concerned with being the best rider on their team than with seeing the team win the race itself. They won't actively work to beat their own teammates, but they are constantly weighing the risks they're willing to take for their team against their own chances of success. For example, when a group of riders breaks free from the pack, a rider in this mind-set will think twice about chasing/bridging because it may hurt his own chances of doing well should he fail. He may be the only one in the right position to react to a threatening move, but he will let it go. Five places have just ridden away with the race, but your team isn't represented because your teammate only wants to beat you.

A more common example: When a breakaway forms containing a teammate, the selfish rider will attempt to bridge across without regard for the situation or the makeup of the group. All he sees is that someone on his team is in the lead, and he responds solely to the threat of losing his stature on the team.

The willingness to sacrifice one's own chances for the good of the team is at the very heart of teamwork. When push comes to shove, will a rider truly make such a sacrifice? If that rider is competing among his own teammates, probably not.

PRACTICING AS A TEAM

How often does your team actually practice a lead-out? How often does your team get together and discuss team tactics? When was the last time you spent a weeknight simply talking or watching bike race videos?

If you're on a normal team, never.

As I mentioned earlier, a very small percentage of teams actually take the time to walk through the tactics in the same way that, say, a football team would walk through a particular play. Very few cycling teams use video cameras to analyze their riding. While NFL teams review film and scout upcoming games, almost no cycling team in America talks about anything on Tuesday nights. Riders would rather spend their Tuesday nights riding as hard as possible until the last bit of daylight leaves the sky. That's fine. There are other nights reserved for easy riding, and those nights should also include time spent in instruction using a dry-erase board and colored markers. Or you can use jargon and hand gestures. Or you can sit at a restaurant table and use those pink, yellow, and white sugar packets to represent riders. To not do it, however, is to make a monumental assumption about the shared knowledge of your teammates.

Generally, teams with strong leaders will carve out the time to go over the basics. They recognize the importance of having everyone on the same page. To them, it is better once in a while to sacrifice a night of riding for a night of classroom lessons.

ASSESSING STRENGTHS AND ASSIGNING ROLES

You thought you were the best sprinter on the team, and then you got your tail whipped by the new guy. (I know that feeling.) Now you must reassign the roles among teammates. If your bruised ego can take it, you would be wise to relegate yourself to the role of lead-out man. There's no shame in that. Mark Renshaw made a tidy living as the lead-out man for Mark Cavendish for a while. He will be the first to tell you that the rush of excitement that comes with delivering your sprinter to the line is pure gold.

As a team grows and develops, roles will change. As new riders join and others leave, roles will change. It's the continual updating and reassessing of those roles that a team must do to improve. When a baseball player is going through a bad hitting slump, the manager may move him around in the lineup. If a golfer can't seem to hit his driver straight to save his life, he may tee off using a three wood instead. There are ways to adjust in every sport. So, too, cycling.

Whoever is leading the team should know the strengths and weaknesses of each rider—not only knowing on a global scale their strengths as sprinters or climbers or time trialists but also knowing who is riding well at a particular point in the season. Individual rider fitness waxes and wanes over the course of a summer. Missing a few days of training here, eating poorly for a few days there, familial commitments scattered throughout the year—these things conspire to create peaks and valleys. Identifying them is an important skill.

On another level, it's good to know whom you can count on when the heat is on. Some riders become invisible when the elbows start to fly. They may have a knack for performing well on Tuesday nights, but they're nowhere to be seen on Sunday.

A strength to look for in teammates is the ability to follow directions and stick to a plan. The roles can change from week to week, but once they're assigned for a particular race, riders need to stick to them. Perhaps you were told to sit on the front and keep everything together

> On another level, it's good to know whom you can count on when the heat is on.

for the first half of the race. If so, stick to that plan. Chase down breakaway attempts; don't bridge across to them. If your role is to stick to the rear wheel of Superman, stick to it.

Too often, riders will agree with every directive during the team meeting, but they'll just "do whatever" when the race is under way.

Here's a real example: Team X had the best sprinter in the land. His nickname was Secretariat. His legs were massive. He was lightning in a bottle. Consequently, he never got into a breakaway because no team was stupid enough to take him along. They knew they would lose.

His team knew this. Their plan was to keep the field together at all costs. They would not let a breakaway get away. Victory was assured if the race finished in a bunch sprint; Secretariat would see to that.

During the first half of the race, the team did a good job of quelling rebellions, as nothing was getting away.

At some point, a small breakaway formed off the front, and a Team X rider went with it. He dutifully sat on the back, refusing to cooperate. But as the break's gap grew, he got a little heady at the idea of being in the winning breakaway and started rotating with the other riders. Soon the breakaway was gone.

With about five laps remaining, guess who fell out of the breakaway? The lone Team X rider. Failure was imminent.

He had found himself in the breakaway, decided to go with it, got cooked, got dropped, and let the top five places get away. Secretariat would end up in sixth place this day.

The rider's first obligation was to keep the breakaway from escaping. His second obligation, when he found himself in the breakaway, was to sit on the back and not do a lick of work to help the breakaway succeed.

Instead, he went off script. I'm sure his team was kind in its post-race analysis.

Stick to your assignments until it becomes obvious that they aren't going to work. If the voices in your head tell you to do something other than what your team discussed before the race started, ignore them.

LEADERSHIP ON THE ROAD

Without leadership, many teams will waste their training time. For instance, they'll spend their easy workout ride hammering along a country road sprinting for city-limit signs. Or they'll simply copy what the strongest rider is doing regardless of whether or not it's right for them. Mostly, they'll try to ride fast all the time. It's a common training mistake to ride too easy on the hard days and too hard on the easy days. Leadership and oversight should force the easy days to be easy. Teams with designated leaders will provide structure and guidance to help maximize the time spent training as a group.

Riding hard, attacking randomly, and sprinting for signs is fine; it's one of my favorite things to do. Some of my best memories of riding involve fierce sprints for the city limit of a town I only visit during club rides. Many tactics might be learned incidentally by doing that. But if a team takes a few minutes after a sprint to talk about what just happened, everyone will learn from what they just did. Learning won't be an accident.

Here's something that you may learn by accident: Not everyone accelerates at the same rate of speed.

During the final laps of a small, unbranded criterium in a nondescript industrial park, I told a teammate to get on my wheel at the start of the final lap; I'd give him a lead-out. He agreed.

As we passed through the start/finish area on the bell lap, I rode up next to him and clicked my brake lever a couple of times to get his attention. Then I took off like a bat out of hell. I passed the front of the field with such speed that no one could see. They were blinded by my contrails. Breathless, I left them. Surely, I thought, I could get him to the final corner without any trouble at all. I kept my eyes on the road and carved the shortest line through the next three corners. I hit the final corner with a full head of steam. This was, undoubtedly, the best lead-out ever.

I hit the exit apex of the final turn and ran out of gas. I looked over my shoulder, expecting to see my teammate zipping up his jersey in preparation for the photo op that was about to happen. Instead, I saw no one on my wheel. I was all alone and out of gas far short of the cantaloupe.

I think I held on for sixth place. They paid to five.

My teammate said I had jumped too hard for him. We had never practiced it on any of our group training rides. We learned it by losing a race. If you add our entry fees to the prize money we could have won, the total cash expense of that lesson was in the neighborhood of $200. Had we worked on it during a training ride, it would have cost us nothing.

If your team is serious about making tactics work, it's not going to happen through osmosis. Someone has to take the lead and play the role of teacher to make sure that your team doesn't fritter away valuable training time. It may require a few rides that include drills, dry runs, and perhaps very little riding (as contradictory as that may sound), but the first time the tactic unfolds in a race the way it's supposed to, you will feel a strange and intoxicating feeling of excitement throughout your body.

That's bike racing.

GROUP TRAINING RIDES

As a competitive cyclist, you will find that most of your time on the bike is spent in solitude. If you're like most roadies, you'll train on your own or in small groups for about 92 percent of your training time. (I just picked that number out of the blue. It sounds pretty accurate, but don't quote me on it.) This accounts for most of your time spent riding out on the open road and on your trainer in the basement. You'll ride alone or with your most trusted riding companion—the one who doesn't half-wheel you to death, the one who attacks you on each climb but waits patiently for you at the top, the one who calls you when it's raining to give you the impression that he wants to ride when he secretly doesn't and is hoping that you'll be the first to chicken out.

Your most trusted riding companion may instead be a power meter, which also doesn't half-wheel you to death but indeed mocks you on the climbs and will ride rain or shine. Either way, you'll have someone or something to push you a little harder. You'll get stronger each time. But as we know by now, stronger doesn't necessarily mean a better racer. It only means that your body is adept at making the bike go fast.

The group ride is where you will become a complete rider. Replicating race dynamics and forcing pack riding skills is the other side of training.

Some clubs have their own exclusive group rides, with outsiders allowed only by invitation. That's a good idea. It allows the club the ability to maintain some level of accountability, and you can exert more control over the things that take place during the ride. Such rides are often overseen by concerned club members who look out for the well-being of the group as a whole. They adhere quite strictly to local motoring laws. They may have a no-drop policy, allowing slower riders to catch up at regular intervals. The pace may be lightning fast or supercasual. As such, if you're going to work on team tactics, this is a good place to do it.

Generally, though, group rides are not restricted in their membership. They are usually open to the cycling public.

Can you feel a good analogy coming on?

Picking the Right Ride

Group training rides are like golf courses. To the untrained eye, they all look alike, though we know they are all different. Even if you play the same golf course twice, it won't be exactly the same both times. Some are easy, and some are wickedly difficult. Some are open to the public; some are private. Some are gorgeously scenic; others not at all.

Some are famous. Some are friendly; some are snooty; most are somewhere in between.

You may think that one big difference between a golf course and a group ride is that a golf course will never expose you to the threat of bodily harm or death the way a group ride will. You've obviously never played Pebble Beach Golf Links, have you? Huge cliffs on hole 8, a par 4 dogleg over water. Crazy.

My point is that all group rides are not alike. They have their own personalities. When looking for a group ride to join, you need to ask more than simply where and when it starts. You need to ask how fast, how far, how aggressive, how safe, how structured, how lame, and how welcoming of newcomers.

Finding the Ride

For new riders who are just starting out, finding the ride is sometimes tricky because a group training ride is kind of like a speakeasy. To find one, you have to ask the right people. Obviously, the best place to start is a local bike shop. They should know where the group rides are. They will likely know of at least one ride on each night of the week, depending on the size of the local cycling community. Smaller communities may have just two or three during the week.

You will spend some time finding the right ride for your ability.

Tuesday-Night Worlds

In most regions, there are regularly scheduled rides that may be hosted by a particular club or bike shop, but participation is open to anyone who knows about it. Again, these rides vary in difficulty and personality. They also vary in the amount of control or structure that is maintained.

Some group rides can be a rambling mess of chaos bordering on criminal; they're Caddyshack on bikes.

Read that last line again. Though simple, it covers a lot of ground. Group rides that are open to all comers within a three-state area tend to draw all types of riders: bulls, tractors, aggressive, passive, experienced, green, friendly, and jerks. Some of these rides are pretty tame and well disciplined. Anyone can join in and get a good workout without much stress or pain. Others, however, are a rambling mess of chaos bordering on criminal; they're *Caddyshack* on bikes. They are notorious for their high speed and no-holds-barred/living-on-the-edge/red-light-running danger, taking up four lanes of traffic and spreading out across a mile of roadway from front to back. Unsanctioned, unlawful, and in many cases unbelievably hard, these rides are the wild, untamed, and uncivilized cousins of sanctioned racing.

Every rider complains about how dangerous these rides are. Every rider vows never to join such a ride ever again. Every rider returns next week with two full water bottles and a pocket full of gels.

One of the most amazing aspects of these Tuesday-Night World Championships, as they've come to be called throughout Roadieland, is how much happens without direction.

Riders in the region just seem to know that the ride begins around 6 p.m., usually in a school or church parking lot. They'll start congregating (sorry) at 5:30 p.m. Without saying a word, some riders will roll out of the parking lot and begin the ride. If you aren't paying attention, you may miss this critical moment. There is no proclamation, no ringing of church bells to signal the start. The ride just rolls when it rolls. To be safe, you'd better have your shoes on and helmet buckled when you step out of the car.

At some indistinguishable point in the first few miles, someone will throw down a huge attack. From that point on, the "go lamp" is lit and will remain ablaze until the end. The exact location of that attack may vary from week to week, but it's usually in the same general area. The instigator may be the same guy, but not always.

Once the pace is high, it will remain high until you get dropped. And make no mistake; you will definitely get dropped unless you happen to be one of the three guys who actually finish this ride. If you're reading this book, you're probably not one of them.

You're on your own to know where the corners, potholes, sprint lines, and mean dogs are located. Someone might point them out to you, but don't count on it. You must also know your own way back to the starting point. This is why GPS was invented, not to direct our troops in battle or to track delivery trucks, as you've been led to believe.

There is no entry fee required and no prize money awarded on this de facto race. It's just a really hard group ride to nowhere. I know of a few rides that award kitsch to the winner. For instance, in south Florida, the infamous Chicken Ride awards a rubber chicken to the winner, who then retains owner- ship of the chicken until the following week. But there is something much more valuable than prizes at stake: pride, glory, status, and respect. Those are what is bestowed, in varying degrees, on the riders who don't get dropped. Nobody really pays attention to who finished in the front group. What gets noticed is who got dropped and when.

Every now and then, a current or former pro rider may show up to partici- pate, which sends a buzz of excitement through the parking lot. Surely, when this happens, everyone will be riding harder than they've ever ridden before. In actuality, the pro was probably looking for a nice, easy night of riding, but he will have to endure countless attacks by mortals testing their mettle against him. He's easy to spot; he's the guy wearing the real team kit, not the one you can buy online.

Here's a little-known fact: USAC's insurance covers all licensed riders during their training rides. However, it only covers training rides that are reg- istered in advance with the federation. This registration requires a fee to be paid for each event.

I think you know what I'm going to say next.

Very few rides in North America pay the fee and buy the coverage. Therefore, you must rely on your personal insurance for anything that hap- pens to you on these rides.

As I said, these group rides are the wild cousin of bike racing, and they exist in various forms almost everywhere.

Not every group ride is this untamed. The Tuesday- (or Wednesday-, or Thursday-) Night Worlds ride is the extreme. You can find less chaotic rides that will fit your mood. But you must know that the simple goal of a group ride is to take you a little farther and a little faster than you've gone before.

It will also teach you etiquette and how to ride safely in a pack. It will definitely tell you where your fitness level is. Warning: You may not like where it is.

Making the Grade

A large group ride that becomes too unwieldy on the road will often split into two groups, cleverly called "the A Group" and "the B Group." In a controlled setting such as the club-sponsored ride, someone may determine which riders may ride with each group based on riding ability, endurance, and strength. This is not an enviable position to be in because few people like to be told that they must ride in the B Group, especially when they feel that they are qualified to ride with the A Group.

In an uncontrolled group, each rider is left to decide for himself which group he belongs in. Choose wisely.

The A Group will naturally be the faster of the two. It has to be that way, or else the earth will spin off its axis and crash into Jupiter.

A common misconception in cycling is that the two groups are separated by speed alone. They are not. Speed is an important part, but they are also separated by all of the abilities I've described in this book: the ability to ride a straight line at a steady speed, the ability to ride through a corner, the ability to rotate through a paceline, the ability to hold on to a wheel even when your face is the color of a radish, and the ability to find the draft and stay in it. Those are the qualities that an A-group rider must have. Going fast is almost an afterthought, a by-product of all those other things. Going fast is also dangerous, so good skills are essential.

The B group is usually a bit more reserved. Speeds are slightly lower. Riders are a lot more vocal about upcoming hazards, turns, cars, and changes in speeds. They may also call out weather conditions, movie reviews, and pork futures. The distance covered may be shorter than that covered by the A group as new riders develop endurance. Though it is not as competitive as the A group, there will still be riders who want to prove that they're the fastest, coolest, and best-looking. They just won't be as fast, as cool, or as good-looking as those in the A group. Ever.

It's important to pick the right group because of the amount of trust necessary at every level of cycling. Riders trust that the rider next to them knows how to do all of the right things on the bike when traveling at high speeds. There is nothing quite as dangerous as a physically strong rider who is in over his head in terms of skill. He may be able to hang on, but he is a menace to everyone's safety.

This is where the challenge of teaching while rolling crops up. Is the offending rider open to instruction? If so, how best to deliver the lesson? Some riders will be very vocal when another rider displays dangerous technique. They might yell. Others will just ride away, leaving the offender to figure it out on his own.

Cycling often gets labeled by outsiders as an elitist sport. The standoffishness that greets a new rider is often misinterpreted as elitism. In fact, it is a matter of personal safety and trust.

This standoffishness is magnified when you join up with a group of strangers with whom you've never ridden. If you do so while the ride is under way, be ready for some heavy scrutiny. As cyclists, we exist within a niche community in which banding together gives us strength and a certain amount of protection. That's cool, but it's always best to get a verbal approval from someone in the group before you join it. Riders generally want to know whom they're riding with.

This etiquette also extends to single riders. Most riders will be happy to have someone to ride with and share the load by drafting, but most appreciate being asked first. There's nothing quite as unnerving as discovering that a wheelsucker has hopped onto your wheel unannounced. What if I stop suddenly? How long has he been there? Why isn't he saying anything? Did he hear me singing that Backstreet Boys song out loud?

Not only do riders want to ride in a safe group, they also prefer to ride with others who are equal to or better than they are in order to elevate their game. This approach is common in many sports. You get better by playing against stronger players, not weaker players. The problem is that at some point a stronger rider will progress past the point of being pushed. When this happens, it's time to find a new group to ride with. And while we all think we'd like to be that strongest rider in the bunch, it's actually not all it's cracked up to be.

I pretend to know.

Traffic Safety

Group rides are open to risks not found in solo rides or sanctioned events. Roads are not closed, intersections are not marshaled, and everyone seems to have a different idea of how the pack should negotiate stops, turns, and motorists.

Beyond the legal ramifications, if an accident occurs during a group ride, the physical and emotional consequences can be devastating. Nobody wants to crash, and no one wants to be responsible for someone else's injury. So the safety of cyclists and motorists should be the number-one priority. It is sheer lunacy to place training above personal safety, yet we see bad habits and practices all the time as riders get caught up in the racelike dynamics on the road.

A good example of this is the attack that launches through a red light or stop sign. Picture a pack of 87 riders approaching a yellow light. The expectation is that we will all stop for the red light. And then one rider attacks through the intersection. He is followed by three or four more riders. Now the race is on, and more riders will take chances to get across the gap.

Another example is the pack that splits as it makes a turn or as a green light changes to yellow and to red. And then there is the pack that makes a left-hand turn off a multilane highway, crossing three lanes to do so.

There is no legal precedent for any of this activity. Local laws make no provision for large groups of cyclists, so it's always a bit of anarchy on our roadways when we ride as a large pack.

I contend—without legal support, I realize—that the best thing to do is to remain one contiguous group throughout any maneuver. Think of your group as a large bus. A bus doesn't split into many smaller pieces when the light turns red; it continues as one unit, just as it did when it left the factory. Motorists are more accepting of one large group than of trying to figure out what several small groups are going to do. The last thing you want is a confused motorist.

Always remember that poor behavior in and around traffic reflects upon your sponsors, your team, and our sport. The law doesn't give a hoot about your training regimen, your city-limit sprint, or your Strava segment. Don't get so lost in your routine that you neglect the laws and paint the cycling community as a band of hooligans.

Once again, communication is the most critical component of a safe ride of any size. Riders must be vocal about cars, potholes, tricky intersections, lane changes, upcoming turns, stops, starts, and generally navigating safely throughout the ride. Once safety is ensured, you can focus on the actual reason you joined the ride: training.

Working as a Team in an Open Group Ride

Working on the fundamentals of team tactics with your own teammates during an open group training ride is possible in the same way that it is possible during a real race. There will be attacks and counterattacks. There will be gaps to bridge, city-limit signs to sprint for, and small groups to work with. It's a great opportunity to work on your verbal and nonverbal communications. The dynamics will be different than in a real race because the general purpose of this type of ride is not to win but to dole out as much punishment as possible.

Oh, sure, you'd like to win the sprint to the next city-limit sign, but the main goal is to not get dropped.

Still, if you keep your objectives simple, you'll be able to get more out of it than just a pair of sore legs. For example, you can work on moving through the pack with a teammate on your wheel as you would if you were leading your sprinter to the front in the final miles. And you can always practice providing your sprinter with a lead-out.

Another phenomenon found on the weekday group rides is the large preponderance of nonracers who participate. The phrase "coming out of the woodwork" applies here. Riders who prefer not to commit to the racing scene on the weekend will get their kicks on the weeknight group training ride.

What are they training for? This. This is what they live for. And make no judgment about it because it's always good to have more people to ride with. Sure, the sport of bike racing would be better if more people attended the actual races, but we have to accept that, for whatever reason, not everyone likes to pay money to get their butt kicked on Sunday when they can have it done for free on Tuesday night.

The allure for them is to test their ability against a known entity. For example, if I'm a nonracer who can outperform or outlast someone who I know is a Cat. IV or Cat. III racer, then I know where I stand athletically. I don't have to be a racer to know where I would finish were I to decide to compete in a real race.

The flaw in this logic is that the racers aren't truly racing, and this isn't a real race. If it were, it would have a different quality entirely, and the outcome would be different.

Don't worry about them as you practice your team tactics. Simply treat them as unknown bike racers whose souls you must crush with your superior skills and tactical know-how.

That is, until you get dropped.

RACING AS A TEAM

For many teams, the race starts with a pre-race meeting that takes place after each rider has had a chance to warm up.

As much as we'd like this to be a time when everyone is focused and paying attention, that is rarely the case. Invariably, someone will be tweaking his bike. Someone will thrust eight safety pins and two race numbers into your hand and expect you to know what happens next. Someone else will be having trouble deciding whether or not to wear arm warmers. Someone else will be filling water bottles (something that should have been done hours before).

That's bike racing. Despite the distractions, this is your best chance to talk about strategies and objectives before the pistol is fired.

At this point, everyone should have a good idea of which pair of legs he brought with him to the race: his never-say-die legs or his who-poured-concrete-into-my-thighs? legs. Here's where you need to be honest in your self-assessment. Your teammates are planning their race based on everyone's input. If you lie about your abilities now, it'll come back to bite you in the behind later. If you're assigned to shadow the Incredible Hulk because you said your legs "feel great," but you only said this because you didn't want to sound weak, good luck. They're now counting on you.

Depending on how advanced your team is, your meeting may consist of just a few comments: "Try not to crash."

A more advanced team may be a little more elaborate: "Let's try to get Chad in the breakaway. If nothing gets away, we'll set up Larry in the sprint."

Who knows? Maybe your team is planning a flash mob during the third lap. That should be discussed before the race. After the race, you can look for new teammates.

There are also some things that you probably shouldn't say at a pre-race meeting. For instance, no one wants to hear you say, "I don't even want to be here."

No one will sympathize if you blurt out, "Gosh, I haven't ridden a single mile in the past month." No one will take you seriously, anyway. That line is used all too often by sandbaggers. It seldom fools anyone. (While it's perfectly acceptable to sandbag when talking to your competition, it is not OK to mislead your own teammates.)

I've heard a story told by racers more than once, and never in a positive way, of a teammate who says, "I'm just going to do my own thing." If you join a team and wear its jersey, the expectation among teammates is that you'll ride as a team unless your team's motto is "Every man for himself."

That motto would look pretty funny on a team jersey because it kind of defeats the purpose of having a team.

"I'll be there for the sprint!" you say.

But will you, really? Or would you be better off doing the early work of keeping the pack together? Are you really able to go fast today? Or are you afraid that someone else on your team will be able to go faster?

The team meeting should also include a breakdown of the prize list to make sure that everyone knows how many places are available. It shouldn't be assumed that everyone knows.

Several years ago, I raced a parking-lot criterium that I was certain paid only to the top five places. I was having one of those rare but lovely days in which I could move easily about the pack without effort. I won a prime easily and had really lively legs, so I should have been in contention at the end. As the final sprint ramped up, I was caught napping. As we rounded the final corner, I looked ahead and counted seven or eight riders in front of me. Thinking that I was in ninth place in a race that paid to the top five, I sat up. Two more riders sprinted passed me. I finished in 11th place.

The race paid to the top 10.

Admittedly, not one of my better performances.

11

GOALS

I STARTED THIS BOOK by talking about motivations. Here we are again. Remember that not everyone has the same motivation for racing, so not everyone has the same goal in mind.

If you could reach your goals without help from anyone else, you wouldn't need a team. But if this is a team sport, and if you do have a realistic goal for the coming season, then you need to share it with your teammates. They should play a part in helping you reach that goal. Maybe it's a particular race. Maybe it's the state championship. Maybe it's something lofty such as a national championship. Or perhaps you just want to gain enough points to upgrade to the next category. Whatever the goals may be, share them. Let the other riders know what you're after and how you'd like them to help you. And also listen to their goals and let them know what you're willing to do to help them achieve them.

Of course, if three riders simultaneously state a desire to be the next state road champion, you might have a difficult time making that work. But at least it's good to get it out in the open.

Once the goals are out on the table, you can start laying out the season and the training that will be required. In fact, you need to. And be thorough in your exploration of all possible roles to help reach those goals. Be supportive of any and all goals within your club. The role of teammate is not limited to the race but includes training and moral support.

The one thing that can kill a team dynamic quickly is selfishness. When riders think only of themselves, they risk alienating their teammates and losing the critical support that they need in a race situation. This is why special attention needs to be given to team-building issues when forming the team and recruiting new riders. Just as we've seen in the pro ranks, inviting a superstar rider to your team may help the team's visibility as a whole, but it might cause conflicts on the road, and it might squash the hopes of some of the lesser riders.

Some riders in this sport have simple, achievable dreams with no one to help them reach them. For instance, a friend once intimated that his goal was to finish a Pro/I/II race in the money. Twentieth place would have made his season a success. He's a person who was on the bottom end of the Cat. II designation due to an impossible work schedule. By all rights, he should have been holding a Cat. III license, but as I mentioned early on, some riders are reluctant to downgrade from their current level. It's a point of pride to hold the highest grade they can, and they're willing to get beat pretty badly while doing so.

It's all relative. A goal such as his is still a goal that will require training and smart riding. Instead of breaking away for the win, 20th place is his 1st place, and he will find himself sprinting against at least 10 other riders who also have their eye on 20th place.

I just hope he does that in a race that pays to 20 places, not 15. That would be disappointing.

To help a guy like that is no different from helping a rider who's trying to win. You must do what's necessary to put him in a position to win that spot. Luckily, bike racing attracts riders who understand that concept and are willing to suffer in order to allow their teammates to succeed. We have a special name for this position: domestique. And we have excellent role models for it: Jens Voigt, Johan Lammerts, Laurens Ten Dam, Frankie Andreu, Chris Horner.

The exploits of these riders are as legendary as those of the riders who give the victory salute. In fact, in my opinion, some of the best pictures in the sporting world are the photos of a rider giving his victory salute while in the background we see his teammates also celebrating, blurred by the camera's shallow depth of field.

Think for a moment of what those riders are willing to do. They sit on the front of the field for hours at a time, holding a pace high enough to discourage attacks. Or they forge to the front in the last kilometers and drive the pace to deliver their rider to the line. Early in their racing career, they showed promise by beating everyone in the county. They rode that talent to the top of the sport. And then, at some point in their climb to the pro peloton, they realized that they belonged in the trenches, slogging out mile after mile for less glory and less money. And that was fine with them.

Luckily, selflessness pays a living wage.

TEAM GOALS

The desire to upgrade to the next level is shared by virtually all bike racers, yet it is rare for a team to dedicate its efforts so that one rider may gain the necessary points. Usually, each rider is left to his or her own devices to collect those points while the team works for its best chance of winning a given race.

I've seen this phenomenon occur many times. A team forms, consisting of four Cat. III riders who vow to work like a real team. We'll call them Athos, Porthos, d'Artagnan, and Frank. Three of them (Athos, Porthos, and d'Artagnan) dedicate themselves every weekend to putting their best rider, Frank, in position to win. By August, Frank has enough points to upgrade to Cat. II, so naturally, he does so.

Meanwhile, Athos, Porthos, and d'Artagnan have little chance of upgrading because their strongest rider is unable to help them; he is now racing in the main event while they languish in the lower category.

They should have adopted the Three Musketeers' motto: "One for all and all for one." When Frank attained the requisite number of points, he should have become a domestique to Athos, Porthos, or d'Artagnan.

In this case, Frank wasn't necessarily selfish. The team simply failed to see the big picture. This type of strategic planning is often overlooked during the course of a season because of all the other things a team must focus on. But if you want to keep a team together, you must consider all angles.

TEAM BUILDING

For more serious teams, racing as a team starts well before the team meeting. It starts in February or March with a weekend (or longer) training camp. This is when a team can spend quality time together and begin to build cohesiveness and a spirit of unity among the riders.

Professional teams usually spend a week in a warm climate. It's often the first chance to spend time with new teammates, receive new clothing and equipment, have team photos taken, and get marching orders for the upcoming season. They'll also conduct some sort of team-building exercise to help them form a bond. Oddly, for many of the bigger pro teams, training camp is the only time of the year when they'll actually see some members of their team. When they break camp, they'll spread to the four corners of the racing world for the next eight months and communicate only through e-mail, text messaging, and Twitter.

Amateur teams hold training camps, too, but they usually involve beer and food and as much riding as they can handle.

For some amateur teams, training camp is the last time they'll speak to each other, not because they'll scatter across the state but because spending too much time in close proximity brings out more drama than a bad episode of *Big Brother*. But these training camps serve the same purpose as a pro team's training camp by bringing the riders together to learn each other's idiosyncrasies. It is highly unlikely that they'll receive their team clothing at this camp because few teams can get their order together that early. And team photos are usually shot with a smartphone app and posted on Facebook, unlike the formal shots of a professional teams.

Seriously, though, your team needs to think and act with the same goal in mind, and it starts right away when you hold your first meeting and start making decisions together. Is it more important for your team's strongest rider to win races? Or do you just want to see your team's kit on the podium, and do you really care who's wearing it? Or are you less interested in winning and more interested in taking home the lion's share of the prize money?

Your collective goals will determine how well you race as a team. As in any partnership, you must accept each other's strengths as well as weaknesses. And then you must, to the best of your ability, hold up your end of the bargain when called upon.

HOW TO WIN, PLACE, OR SHOW

There's no real secret to winning a race. You just need to beat all of the other guys. To beat the other guys, you have to put yourself on a higher plane when it comes to nerves, commitment, and resolve. Beyond the pedaling of the bike and working with teammates, when discussing the actual winning (or placing) in a bike race, it comes down to what's upstairs.

Golf, if played correctly, is an intense activity that requires certain amounts of athletic prowess and muscular control and a great amount of concentration. For almost five hours, a golfer must have laserlike focus on each shot. That is, if he's trying to shoot a decent score. I like to use golf as an example because it is usually regarded by nongolfers as the least taxing sport ever invented, but playing your best round can leave you feeling like a noodle walking off the 18th green.

Racing in an important race should be as demanding mentally as it is physically. If you're engaged in every moment of the race, it will drain you. If you're serious about performing well, prepare your mind as much as your legs.

Going for It

What separates a good rider from one with great results varies according to his or her level of dedication and ability. For a rider who is both strong and dedicated, it boils down to a matter of self-belief. The hackneyed sports adage "If you can believe it, you can achieve it" isn't entirely accurate here. Believing I can win the National Championship Road Race is one thing; beating 120 of America's best riders is another. We are all dedicated and strong. There is more to it.

A better way to say it, then, might be "If you don't believe it, you'll never achieve it." On top of having the tools, I have to believe that it's possible for me to win the national championship.

(For the record, I have no such delusions.)

Riders who win have no doubt about their ability to do so. They don't go into a race thinking "I'll be lucky if I finish in the top 10." No, they believe "If everything goes well, I can win this."

When crunch time comes in the last few laps of a criterium, you must ask yourself, "Do I really want it, and do I feel I deserve it?" The answer will determine whether or not you're going to squeeze through small gaps between riders, make contact without flinching, and dig deeper than you ever do on training rides because there will come a point in the process where you draw the line between trying harder and just accepting what you've accomplished so far. Not everybody answers that call the same way. Some riders are satisfied with just doing well.

Very few successful racers approach the finish line recklessly. It's a highly calculated effort weighing a lot of thoughts at once. At some point in the race, they had an inner monologue that went something like: "I'm in a good position here; how am I going to win this race?" The finish usually sorts it all out, and everyone ends up pretty close to where he should be in the final results.

All else being equal, it's the self-believers who have the advantage.

Some riders are always in the hunt for the top step, not simply because they have strong legs but because the fire burns hot all the time, and they believe that they belong among the top finishers. Pro riders are paid to want it whether they truly want it or not. But generally, they want it. If they didn't, they'd become civil engineers or anvil salesmen.

Try this during your next race: Turn off your power meter. Put tape over your speedometer. Don't look at your heart rate.

The numbers that appear on your device can't measure intestinal fortitude. The power meter can only display your wattage, speed, heart rate, and mileage; it can't display the fire in your belly. Bike racing relies on that fire. If you start believing the numbers, you may back down.

When speedometers became popular in the 1980s, my team coach, Jeff Noftz, discouraged younger riders from using them in a race. He knew that we would see speeds we had never seen during training. He was right. In a popular race on Erie Street in Windsor, Ontario, I saw numbers I had seen only on steep descents. It was unsettling. I had to force myself to look away and ignore what I had just seen. Never in any of our training rides had I seen 34 mph while on level ground, but here I was, bumping elbows at that speed.

Luck

When you can't count on your inner fire to drive you to the line, there's always luck. If you're going to be a bike racer, you'll experience plenty of luck, both good and bad. Never count on the good kind, but be ready to capitalize when it presents an opportunity. Accept the bad kind as it comes. Nothing personal, my friend.

Every now and then the skies part, and fortune (good for some, bad for others) plays a lead role.

In the final laps of the 1991 National Criterium Championship race in Salt Lake City, Sherri Rodgers-Kain was on the verge of exhaustion while stronger riders were ramping up the pace for the final sprint. She was at the back of the pack, just trying to hang on. In fact, she had considered dropping out but held on because she didn't want to let her sponsors down. And then, with just eight laps to go, a large crash caused half of the field to be knocked to the floor. It was standard-issue race mayhem, with bikes and bodies strewn across the road. Officials were forced to neutralize the race until all injured riders could be treated and removed from the course. The delay lasted 20 minutes. The field of riders continued to tool around at 15 mph while the course was cleared. All the while, Sherri rested.

By the time racing had resumed, she had recovered and was able to sprint to win the national championship. She was lucky to be given the opportunity to rest. She still had to beat all the others who had also rested, but the delay was what saved her.

I don't know how many times I've seen crashes occur on the very last lap of a criterium. I never kept track of the actual number, but I know it happens a lot. All that tension that I spoke of a few pages ago sometimes goes awry, and riders get taken out of the race at the worst possible time.

Don't let that discourage you from racing your bike. If you know it's a possibility, watch out for it. And know that it doesn't always have to be bad.

As a racer, I've benefited from final-lap crashes on a couple of occasions. In West Carrolton, Ohio, I was riding at the back of a large field and, like Sherri, had written off any chance of grabbing a place on the prize list. It's hard to win from the tailgunner's position. But I had concerns about a dicey left-hand turn on the back side of the course; during the race, more than one rider had ended up in the homeowner's front yard.

On the last lap, the pack became bunched up as everyone crowded to be at the front. Of course, the speed was high. The little hairs on the back of my neck stood at attention. In preparation for the inevitable, I moved to the left side of the road as we approached the left-hand turn. We all know what happens when a crash occurs on a left-hand turn. Centrifugal force is going to dump everyone in the right gutter.

It did. A huge crash swept 90 percent of the field into the same front yard as before. Magically, my small band of fellow tailgunners had a clear shot at the finish line. I surely didn't win, but I remember cashing a check for $10, which is $10 more than I was due.

I will not list the many ways that bad luck can ruin your race. If you've spent more than six weeks in the sport, you've already started compiling your own list. Again, it's part of bike racing, and what you make of those opportunities is up to you.

When another rider suffers bad luck, you have a choice to make: Cut him some slack, or capitalize on it.

Many debates have been held as to whether or not Alberto Contador should have attacked Andy Schleck during the 2010 Tour de France when Schleck dropped his chain on a climb. Some say Contador should have been a gentleman and waited. Others say he was right to attack. When another rider suffers bad luck, you have a choice to make: Cut him some slack, or capitalize on it. It depends on which school you come from—or what kind of mood you're in.

Bikes break. Tires go flat. Riders bonk. Spouses accept invitations to baby showers on the wrong day. That's bike racing. Sometimes other people's bikes break, their tires go flat, they bonk, and so on. That's bike racing, too. Be ready.

Chris Horner   OLYMPIC BAD LUCK

A professional athlete always has to be prepared for bad luck. It's bound to happen to everyone, and in professional sports—especially bike racing— it's impossible to avoid. I've spent 20 years trying to make the U.S. Olympic team, and at 41 years of age, I was finally getting my first chance in 2012.

I had just finished 13th at the Tour de France, and the next day I was heading off to represent the United States in the London Olympic Games. My bike sponsor had sent a custom-painted USA Olympic bike specifically for the race, and I got to ride it for the first time when I arrived in London. As I was riding it during training, I kept complaining to the mechanics every time I returned that the brakes didn't seem to be functioning at the same level as those on my Tour de France bike. The mechanics kept reassuring me that everything had been checked with the bike, and it was working fine. By the time the race rolled around a few days later, I had started to believe that it was just me, or possibly the wheels I had been using for training, which were different from the race wheels I had been using during the Tour de France.

→

SPLITTING THE WINNINGS

They were the best of friends until one of them won a bike race. After that, they never spoke.

Sound familiar? It's happened more than once in this sport: two riders disagreeing on how the winnings should be divided. It strains their friendship past the breaking point. This is one of the more interesting aspects of bike racing that isn't found in other sports, mainly because few other sports require such intense effort and offer cash prizes to the top finishers. In a softball

OLYMPIC BAD LUCK, CONTINUED

When the Olympic race started, I was the first to attack at mile 10. I had flown into the first hard, almost 180-degree turn with a small gap, and as I went to grab the brakes for the first time at race speed, my intuitions proved to be correct. The bike slowed at nowhere near the rate of my Tour de France bike, and suddenly I knew I had no chance of making the corner. I flew off into the crowd, landing on the fans standing 20 deep on that section of road.

After getting back into the race, I decided that it was best to switch back to my Tour de France bike. Right away, I felt at home and back in my element. However, an hour and a half after I resumed racing on the Tour bike, my left-side crankarm fell off. Suddenly, I was standing on the side of the road, holding one crankarm with my pedal still attached to it up in the air, hoping that the team mechanic would understand that this was the code for "Bring my Olympic bike back!" Even though it had taken me 20 years to get there, the one good thing was that at this age, I could appreciate the experience of the Olympics and understand that sometimes bad things just happen. ◼

league, the winning team often gets T-shirts, and the trophy ends up collecting dust in a bar or a closet somewhere. In cycling, we usually pool all of our winnings, primes, and any loose coins we find in the parking lot and then decide who gets what based on the amount of work he or she did in the race and how effective that work was.

And we do this with teammates we aren't even sure participated in the racing. Being in the race and being involved in the race are two different things.

The Payout

On the rare occasion that I find myself in a breakaway, I assume that all of my teammates are working diligently at the front of the field to preserve my lead and prevent any chase efforts, but I can't actually see it happen. For all I know, they could be sitting on the back of the pack, telling ghost stories they learned at summer camp. But after the race, they'll assure me that they turned themselves inside out to help.

Do I share my prize money? Yes.

How much? I don't know. Knowing me, I probably finished in fifth place, so we're not dividing a pot of gold. More like a $25 gift card and a set of tires.

Still, I've seen grown men have hissy fits over an amount of money that doesn't even begin to pay for the gas money to get there. Obviously, it's not about the money; it's the principle.

The true payout of this sport boils down to appreciation and respect. Most riders just want a little love for the effort. Yes, some will only accept that love in legal U.S. tender—nothing smaller than a twenty, thank you—but most riders just want to be appreciated for what they've done. And what they've done is considerable. Remember how much work is involved with blocking and chasing and the sacrifice necessary to make it happen.

The true payout of this sport boils down to appreciation and respect.

A much more experienced friend of mine once said something to the effect of "I'll bury myself to help a teammate win, and he doesn't have to pay me a nickel. But if he doesn't at least thank me, I'll have to think twice about working that hard for him again."

I cleaned that up a little. He spoke in bike racer language that's probably too spicy for these pages.

I've heard the same sentiment from other riders on more than one occasion. It's a commonly held desire to simply be thanked.

An Honest Assessment of Your Contribution

If you never saw the front of the field, you probably didn't influence much of what happened in the course of the race and as such probably didn't contribute much to the overall success of your team.

Near the front of the peloton is always a good place to ride, but the actions involved in contributing occur in the front three or four places. There is little you can do to affect the outcome of the race by sitting in 9th or 10th position. Perhaps you can tow a teammate to the front, allowing him to save his energy for a breakaway. Or maybe you will launch him into an attack. You may retrieve water bottles from the team car. In these cases, you will play a part without actually reaching the front lines of the battle. But generally, in amateur racing, the contributions are a bit more hands-on.

If, after the race, you find yourself waiting to receive money from your teammates who actually receive prize money, you need to be honest about how much of a part you played in the outcome. Just showing up for the race and wearing a clean jersey doesn't guarantee a payday.

Although it might.

Some teams, in an attempt to reduce the number of hissy fits, make it a policy that all prize money is evenly divided among all riders who enter the race, regardless of what transpired during said race. If so, start making plans on how to spend your $12. Dream big. New tubes? Bar end plugs? The possibilities are endless.

Even if your club has a policy that governs this, it should allow you the ability to opt out of any profit sharing. If you're able to openly admit that you never saw anything but rear ends all day, speak up.

Sure, this sport is pricey, and it's always hard to turn down free money (although any money won in a bike race is anything but free).

But be honest with yourself and your teammates. If you weren't up there during the race, they'll know it. And so will you.

PEP TALK

I recently raced on a very cold and windy day. The flags were as straight as plywood. The temperature was in the 30s. I was wearing four layers of clothing during my warm-up. When I opened my jar of embrocation, I could have sworn I heard it whimper.

As we were getting dressed, my teammates were playing the lower-our-expectations game, filling their heads with negative thoughts and negative talk.

"I'm not looking forward to this."

"Man, I don't want to be here."

"I'm not feeling well. I may just ride the first half."

"This sucks."

As you may have guessed, our race was over before it began. We fed off each other's negativity as we commiserated about the conditions. As a result, we struggled to put one rider in the breakaway. Half of our team didn't finish the race. We didn't have any fun. We would have been better off playing cards that day.

Instead of going that route, we should envision Belgium. We should grit our teeth and attack the day, grab it by the throat, and make it our slave.

It's a natural game that we cyclists play to try to lower our expectations. The problem is, we usually end up lowering our tolerance, and we simply knuckle under.

Never talk yourself out of it. Do what you came to do: Race your bike.

12

GO RACE

NOW, ARMED WITH A FULL SET of skills and tactics, approach your next race with confidence.

Let nothing take you by surprise. Be ready for the attack that comes in the first lap, even though the odds of its succeeding are low. Keep your eyes on Crazy Dave each time he goes on a bungee attack; you never know when he'll become Joop Zoetemelk. Anticipate the rider who blocks for his wife's brother who rides for a different team. Be ready when the breakaway gets reeled in. Be ready when the violins start playing a high-pitched minor chord that makes the hair on the back of your neck stand up. Be proactive, not reactive, in your approach to tactics.

Be patient. The race is rarely won in the first turn. Rarely does the first breakaway attempt succeed. Most of the real racing comes in the second half of the race. The final kilometer is a lot longer than you think. There's another race next weekend.

Approach the next race with confidence. By now, you have the skills to do more than simply follow the wheel in front of you. You know how to get through each turn without losing five places, how to handle whatever Mother Nature throws at you, how to save your energy for when it's really needed, and how to be in the right position when the peloton reaches the bottom of the first climb.

Study bike racing. Become a student of the sport. Watch a race, not only to see who wins but to see which teams make mistakes. There is as much to be learned by watching not-so-good teams do it wrong as there is by watching the good teams do it right. You can learn a lot from watching a pro race, but remember that you will need to make adjustments when applying what you learn to your own pack of Cat. III riders.

Practice to improve your weaknesses and race to your strengths. Don't learn just one trick and use it at every race. Develop a bag of tricks. Never let your competition become so familiar with your racing style and abilities that they can predict your every move. Though it's more fun to practice the things that you're good at, don't develop blind spots by ignoring your weaknesses. They're not going to go away on their own. They will be exploited.

Take command of your team. Be the rider on your team who initiates conversations of tactics whether it's through e-mail, at the coffee shop, or in the car to and from races. Get your teammates talking about different roles and responsibilities. Don't let them fall into the every-man-for-himself mentality that so many teams lapse into.

Find your motivation. One thing about bike racing that is certain: You will constantly amaze yourself by how much harder you can push yourself with the right motivation. You have a deeper tank than you think. Learn to motivate yourself, and you'll find a way to stay on the wheel in front of you.

Prepare to be yelled at. Your fellow racers love you dearly, but they will yell when you do something that threatens their well-being or disrupts the magic of a ride, whether it's opening a gap in the middle of a paceline, taking a bad line through a turn, or attacking in the feed zone. Don't take it personally; we're not being mean. Mostly, it's a function of shouting over the rushing wind combined with the need for immediacy. Under calm circumstances, we will teach. In battle, we will yell.

Keep it all in perspective. We're not racing for interplanetary supremacy here. Though I suggest that you need to be fearless when sticking your handlebar into tight spaces, I hope you'll keep both feet on the ground in the heat of battle. Most of us have to return to the real world on Monday morning with all 206 bones intact. Race your best without being reckless. Also accept the fact that you may not have the genetic makings of a champion and that no injection, transfusion, or pill can ever be justified in bridging the gap.

Be ready for the fame of winning. Go ahead and practice your victory salute. If all goes well, you may get to use it soon. Just remember that the rules require that you keep one hand on the handlebar at all times. Still, you can get pretty creative with a one-handed salute. You might also practice the equally popular second-place-rider-pounding-his-handlebar-in-frustration move just in case this book fails to help. You can't win 'em all.

//

It doesn't matter why you come to the starting line on Sunday. The fact is, you're there. If you had fun before, I'm hopeful that you'll have even more fun now. If you've been successful, perhaps you'll bring home more free stuff. If you've started to lose interest, maybe this will kick you in the butt to get excited again.

Whatever your motivation . . .

Go race.

PHRASEOLOGY

In my first season of Little League baseball, my coach instructed me to "choke up." Eager to please, I did my best to become verklempt. But my misty eyes prevented me from seeing the ball, so I struck out on three straight pitches. I later learned what "choke up" really means in baseball.

Baseball has the screwgie, tater, and dinger. Volleyball has the dink, roof, and pancake. Surfing has goofy-foot, grommet, and sand facial.

Like any activity worth pursuing, bike racing comes with its own lingo—words and phrases that may mean one thing in the normal world but mean something wholly different in the cycling world.

Here's a partial list of what cycling brings to *The Dictionary of Usually Useful Sport Phrases.*

Arrivée. This word shows up in most cycling glossaries, though I've never actually seen it used at an American bike race. It's a French word that means the finish line. I'll use it in a sentence for you: You'll probably never see "arrivée" used on a finish line banner in the United States.

Attack. A sudden and preferably unexpected acceleration by one rider with intentions of breaking free of the bunch, either alone or with help. There will be several of these during your next race. With any luck, one will be yours.

Baked. Someone who is overtrained, as indicated by a large dip in performance during the peak of racing season. The rider becomes discouraged by his poor results, so he mistakenly trains harder when the opposite is needed. The body needs rest, but the brain has a hard time accepting this.

Bonk. If you are unable to take on food or drink while riding, you will likely receive a visit from the bonk fairies, who replace cyclists' muscles with wet noodles. The bonk is simply a depletion of blood glucose that robs you of energy, stemming from failure to eat while riding. For this, we have an adage: Eat before you're hungry. Drink before you're thirsty. Don't crash when you do either.

Boxed in. Getting stuck in the middle of the group with no escape route at a key moment in the race. Someone may be doing it to you intentionally, or it may be your own inattentiveness that put you in a bad position. "Two hundred meters from the line, I got boxed in. I was all, like, 'Move over! Let me out,' but they were, like, not moving. So I was, like, lucky to break the top 20."

Break du Jour. In big stage races, the breakaway that gains a large advantage, forays off the front for a majority of the race, and is almost always caught in the last few miles. Rarely seen in American amateur bike races.

Bunch. *Also* **Field, Group, Pack, Peloton.** The largest group of riders in a bike race is called by any of these names. There is no special context in which one is used over another. If the field breaks into several parts, we simply call them groups: lead group, chase group, third group, and so on.

Bunny Hop. A quick jump of rider and bicycle over a small obstacle. A bunny hop is a handy skill to clear railroad tracks or junk that might cause a flat tire, and it's fine to use when you're riding solo. But in a paceline, bunny hopping over a pothole without warning is one of the worst things you can do to the riders behind you. The preferred method is to call out all obstacles (potholes, road kill, detritus, flotsam, jetsam, etc.) while moving to one side so that everyone else can see it and miss it. Calling out is done as a common courtesy when the race is traveling at a mellow pace. It is optional, though appreciated, when the racing gets serious.

Category, or Cat. USA Cycling's official racing classification for amateurs based upon results and experience. Men's road racing has five categories, starting with Category V for beginners and progressing to Cat. I for top riders. The system is the same for women's racing, except that there are only four categories.

Combine. An ad hoc team that you will be forced to recruit when your real teammates neglect to inform you that they're not driving 6 hours to Timbuktu to race a 20-minute crit.

Cover. When riding in support of a stronger teammate, your job may be to ride near the front and respond to (cover) any attacks that go up the road. "Dave, your job is to sit at the front and cover. Don't do any work. Just sit on."

Criterium, or Crit. A short race that your family will not willingly attend. A criterium is a race of many laps held on a short course closed to vehicular (and, with alert course marshals, pedestrian) traffic. Not to be confused with a road race or a time trial, which your family will also not willingly attend.

DFL. Last place. Dead last. The *F* is added for emphasis.

"DFL" only refers to the final results. It's entirely possible to ride in last place for the entire race and still win.

Oddly, DFL is not exclusive to the last-placed rider. Any rider who finished in the tail end of the pack may refer to himself as DFL, usually with a certain degree of self-loathing. Thus the addition of the *F*.

DNF. Did not finish. You either quit or crashed out or were asked to retire by the race officials because you were too far out of contention to worry about.

DNS. Did not start. This three-letter designation seldom shows up in amateur racing because amateur riders rarely waste money registering for a race in which they won't compete. Something pretty drastic must occur to prevent a rider from starting a race. It could be as drastic as a kid's birthday party or a spouse's body language.

Drill It. *Also* **Bury It, Push It.** Set a torrid pace. "With 2 kilometers to go, we need Larry to go to the front and drill it."

Dropped. *Also* **Shelled, Cooked, Flicked, Fried, Spit out the Back.** Various words to indicate that someone has been left behind by the peloton. When read together, these words seem to involve seafood. That's not the case.

    Other popular terms meaning the same thing include "blow up," "explode," "pop," "crack," "go backward," and "knackered." Not to be confused with the bonk (*see* Bonk), these terms refer to a lack of fitness or mental toughness, whereas the bonk is caused by a real physiological change.

Escape. Journey's last great album.

Feed Zone. The feed zone is a designated area along the course where you get a hand-up of food and drink. It takes a certain skill to take a hand-up from your soigneur while you're riding through the feed zone at 20 mph. It's a technique you must practice if you want to avoid crashing. On the bright side, if you crash in the feed zone, there is a car right there to carry your broken bike back to the start/finish area.

Field Fodder. If you never take a flyer (*see* Flyer), if you never chase an attack, if you never win prize money, if you never participate in the racing that happens at the front of the peloton, if you never see the front of the peloton, you will be considered to be field fodder, or pack fodder. This is more a descriptive than a derogatory term. Well, actually, it's both.

Field Sprint. Despite your repeated efforts to form a breakaway group, the field is going to finish all together. This becomes a field sprint. It's very entertaining for the spectators but nerve-wracking for the racers.

Flyer. A solo attack. A gutsy move that is as often doomed as it is successful. If you go on even one flyer per season, you will be considered an aggressive rider.

Fred. *Also* **Cat. VII, Jaboffo.** Like every other sport, bike racing has words to describe riders who are new and inexperienced, who focus a little too much on the technical aspects, or who are simply slow on the uptake.

Fred and Frieda are cycling's lovable nerds, identified by the three computers mounted to their handlebars, a helmet mirror, and a fascination with reflective tape.

"Cat. VII" refers to riders who are so new to the sport that they haven't yet reached Cat. V status (which is as simple as filling out a form online). Interestingly, there is seldom mention of Cat. VI, which would be the logical step before Cat. V, but most people actually jump to Cat. VII to emphasize just how new this rider is.

"Jaboffo" is a phrase that has been around since the 1970s. It denotes a rider who has yet to master the necessary skills but is seemingly unaware of this fact.

Get on a Wheel. *Also* **Stay on a Wheel, Follow a Wheel, Hold a Wheel.** To be on someone's wheel means that you're in their draft. Your success in this sport will hinge on your ability to find the draft, get in the draft, and stay there and hold it. If you're a beginner, getting on a wheel can be unnerving because you must ride so close to the rider in front of you in order to benefit from the draft.

Glued to a Wheel, Glued to the Rim. These two phrases sound similar but mean vastly different things. "Glued to a wheel" means to stay in contact with one specific rider relentlessly. "I wasn't going to let Ray go up the road without me. I was glued to his wheel for the whole race." (I can promise that Ray found this annoying.) "Glued to the rim" is how tubular tires are affixed to the wheel's surface.

Hammer. *Also* **Animal, Diesel, Driver, Horse, Motor, Specimen.** Anyone who can sit on the front of the pack and hold an uncomfortably high pace for long periods of time without talking. They probably can't climb or sprint particularly well, but they can ride harder than average for longer than you want them to.

"That guy is a hammer. He sat on the front for 4 miles without pulling off."

"Hammer" and "motor" can also be used as verbs: "It's slightly downhill, so you can just motor through that section of the course and then hammer on the flat."

Hook. To impede someone's forward progress by moving into their line in a brutish manner. In cycling lingo, I "have position on you" if my handlebars and shoulders are ahead of yours, and therefore I have the right of way. It doesn't mean I can do whatever I want; I must continue to ride a reasonably predictable and safe line. However, I don't have to consider your feelings when I do this. And if I really want to halt your forward progress, I can simply move over into your line. This is most effective if I pin you up against the curb, thus preventing your escape. If I do this slowly, it's cool. If I do this abruptly, it's not so cool. It's dangerous. That's a hook. Eddie B. would have totally dug this in 1984. We dig it a lot less nowadays.

Another use of the word "hook" is to literally hook handlebars together. This will spike your heart rate in a hurry. Pull apart too quickly and you will probably crash. The best way to mitigate this is to relax and hope for a miracle. (Relaxing is always your best option.) To prevent it altogether, ride with your hands in the drops when you're in close proximity.

HTFU. The *H* stands for Harden. The *U* stands for Up. The *T* means The, and the *F* adds emphasis. This endearing term is used by fellow riders as encouragement for you to overcome your delicate upbringing, at least temporarily.

KOM, QOM. King of the Mountains, Queen of the Mountains. A prize for the best climber of the race. Points are awarded to the top three or five riders to reach the top of designated climbs. Whoever receives the most points wins the title of "King" or "Queen of the Mountains." Why anyone would want this is beyond me; they make you wear polka dots.

LBS. Local bike shop. You can buy anything online for a lower price, but if you want it right now and you want it to fit correctly, you need an LBS. It's smart to establish a friendly relationship with the people who work at an LBS because you will someday find yourself banging on their door at 6:05 on Friday night because you need a new inner tube before your 8 a.m. race the next day. If you're the sort of customer who buys everything online, they may not hear you knocking.

Lead-out. A tactic in which your team's designated sprinter stays tucked in the draft of his or her teammates as they accelerate to the finish line in the final mile of the race. In a successful lead-out, the sprinter turns on the afterburners with 100 meters to go and wins the race.

"My teammates gave me a sweet lead-out. All I had to do was stay upright, and I had the win."

And guess who's buying dinner.

Line. A presumed path of travel. Anything that varies from this path will elicit comments from affected riders. If the pack is zigzagging its way along the home stretch, that's fine. But if one rider zigs while the rest zag, you'll hear someone shout, "Hey, hold your line!" *See also* Stick.

Miles. Fitness. For a cyclist, fitness comes by riding lots of miles. There's really no faking it. Someone who isn't in shape will say, "I just don't have the miles to hang with the fast group."

They may be lying; *see* Sandbagger.

n + 1. The ideal number of bikes to own. Johnny currently owns seven bikes. Therefore, n = 7.

Johnny then discovers that seven bikes is not enough. He needs how many more to be happy? One.

Johnny currently owns eight bikes. . . .

No-Man's-Land. Located somewhere in the gap between the field and the breakaway. You will die a slow and lonely death if you run out of gas halfway across the gap. That's why it's important to know your optimal bridging distance—the distance that you know you can cover in one big effort.

Off the Front. *Also* **Gone, Rode Away, Up the Road.** Whenever a group of riders gets a lead, no matter how small, it's considered a breakaway. If the gap is small, it's just a gap "off the front." If the group rides away into the sunset, we use the other phrases to say so. By the way, even though the finish line is found somewhere down the road, a breakaway always goes "up the road." Even if the route is entirely downhill, the break goes up the road. In 30-plus years of cycling, I've never heard of a breakaway going down the road.

OTB. Off the back. No longer in contact with the peloton because you're going too slow. We never use "OTF" to denote being off the front, nor does it mean "on the front." It just doesn't have the same ring to it.

Palmarès. Your personal list of cycling accomplishments. "The Athens Twilight Criterium victory was the first nighttime win in his palmarès." This is another French word that you almost never hear at American races, mainly because no one is exactly sure how to pronounce it, but you may spot it in a magazine once in a while. Or on page 50.

Peloton. Cycling's most formal name for the bunch. We also sometimes use "peloton" to indicate the sport in general: "He's one of the most respected riders in the peloton."

Prime. Pronounced "preem." An intermediate prize awarded at some random point in a criterium at the discretion of the promoter, officials, or announcer. A prime lap is a single-lap race within a race. The announcer makes the announcement, a bell is rung, and whoever wins that particular lap wins the prime. Primes can be cash or merchandise. Listen closely to what the announcer is saying. Always.

Pull. If you're the first rider in a paceline, you're said to be pulling. "Taking a pull" means that you're taking your turn at the front, allowing others to ride in your draft. If you're the only one willing to do this, you'll end up towing or dragging everyone along with you. "Jason was pulling at the front and then tried to get across the gap to the leaders but ended up towing the entire field up with him."

Pull It Back. *Also* **Chase It Down, Close the Gap, Reel It In, Shut It Down.** To catch the breakaway. Also, possible names for an album by a rock band.

Punching Tickets. Someone who rides at the back of the pack but never gets dropped punches tickets. As other riders get dropped, they get their imaginary tickets punched by this rider before they go OTB. I don't know where the phrase originated or even what it even means, but I've punched a lot of tickets during my racing career.

Rain Bike. *Also* **Beater.** The first bike you ever own will be your pride and joy. It will reside in the living room under special spotlights to highlight its beauty. Every component on it will be perfectly matched to create the perfect ride. It's hard to believe that at some point, this paragon of perfection will be scratched, dinged, and cobbled together using a mishmash of various components. This will then become the beater bike that you ride in the rain or on dirt roads because your newest bike will obviously melt when exposed to water and mud. Plus, it's on display in your living room.

Red Kite. Another romantic notion that never makes it to American races. In Europe, they hang a red pennant over the road to mark 1 kilometer from the finish. At most races in the United States, they'll set up a sign that the wind will knock over long before the peloton ever sees it.

Road Rash. That long scrape of torn flesh you acquired by crashing.

Roubaix Face. The default contorted facial expression of all racers when the pace is staggering. Teeth bared, mouth agape, eyes squinting, and head cocked to one side. Very flattering.

Rouleur. A rider with a smooth, powerful, even cadence who can seemingly keep it going all day.

Sandbagger. Someone who constantly downplays his or her ability, desire, or fitness level in the hope of being disregarded when the race is on. Also, riders who intentionally remain in a lower category despite having the requisite points to upgrade.

Sit In, Sit On. There is a subtle difference between "sitting in" and "sitting on."

If you are in the slipstream of others, you are sitting in. If you are in the slipstream of others with the intent of advancing your position at their expense or with no intention of helping, you are sitting on.

"I sat in for the entire race." This means that you were either lazy or unable to contribute. You rode the same distance, but you didn't really race much. When the finish line came, you were just happy to be there.

"I sat on and let them tow me to the finish." You refused to contribute. When the finish line came, you sprinted around the riders who towed you.

You can also sit on the front if you're so inclined: "Larry sat on the front and motored for five laps."

Soigneur. When you become a professional racer, you will have servants and slaves to attend to your every whim and feed you grapes while fanning you with palm fronds because that's what a soigneur does. Until then, anyone who helps you keep your camp in order will be a family member or really good significant other. As they stand in the hot sun for hours to hand you food and bottles, pack the car while you kibitz with your teammates, and console you on yet another tough loss, they are collecting points that they will redeem later. Live it up.

Sprinter. Someone who can go really fast in a crowd of others when the time comes. It's a special talent. This rider is like a diva in the opera who can hit the high notes. You don't dare ask him or her to do anything else.

Stagiaire. An amateur rider who joins a pro team for part of a season to gain experience. Hey, it happens.

Steed, Stable. Some roadies refer to their bike as a "steed" and their collection of bikes as their "stable." I laugh every time I hear it. What are we? A Renaissance festival? Zounds!

Stick. A command that originated on the velodrome that's a more succinct way to say, "Hold your line." It is seldom said calmly.

Tailgunning. Sitting at the back of the pack.

Track Hack. A cough that comes from riding a really hard race. The phrase is stolen from the world of track racing, but it applies to cycling in general, where racing tends to stress the lungs.

Turning Squares. Refers to the pedaling action of riders who are cooked and have lost all fluidity in their pedal stroke. The pedals still travel in a round motion, but you'd never know it by looking at the legs.

Wheelsucker. Someone who seldom works (*see* Work). Not a term of endearment.

Work. To contribute to the speed of a race. Even if you never go off the front, place in the money, or enjoy any success in a race, you will still earn the respect of others if you do some work during the race. It's funny, but racers keep track of this sort of thing.

"I sat in all day; I didn't do any work."

Yeah, we know.

Yellow Jersey. The yellow jersey is, of course, what the leader of the Tour de France wears to make him easy to spot as the pack flies by at 30 mph. The French term is *maillot jaune*. Yellow is the most popular color for leader's jerseys throughout the world except at the Tour of Italy, where the yellow jersey is pink. Or, as they say in Italy, "In France, the pink jersey is yellow."

GEAR CHART

NUMBER OF TEETH ON FRONT CHAINRING

	27	28	29	30	31	32	33	34	35	36	37	38	39	40	41	42
11	65	67	70	72	74	77	79	82	84	86	89	91	94	96	98	101
12	59	62	64	66	68	70	73	75	77	79	81	84	86	88	90	92
13	55	57	59	61	63	65	67	69	71	73	75	77	79	81	83	85
14	51	53	55	57	58	60	62	64	66	68	70	72	73	75	77	79
15	47	49	51	53	55	56	58	60	62	63	65	67	69	70	72	74
16	45	46	48	49	51	53	54	56	58	59	61	63	64	66	68	69
17	42	43	45	47	48	50	51	53	54	56	57	59	61	62	64	65
18	40	41	42	44	45	47	48	50	51	53	54	56	57	59	60	62
19	37	39	40	42	43	44	46	47	49	50	51	53	54	56	57	58
20	36	37	38	40	41	42	44	45	46	47	49	50	51	53	54	55
21	34	35	36	38	39	40	41	43	44	45	46	48	49	50	51	53
22	32	34	35	36	37	38	40	41	42	43	44	46	47	48	49	50
23	31	32	33	34	36	37	38	39	40	41	42	44	45	46	47	48
24	30	31	32	33	34	35	36	37	38	40	41	42	43	44	45	46
25	28	30	31	32	33	34	35	36	37	38	39	40	41	42	43	44
26	27	28	29	30	31	32	33	34	36	37	38	39	40	41	42	43
27	26	27	28	29	30	31	32	33	34	35	36	37	38	39	40	41
28	25	26	27	28	29	30	31	32	33	34	35	36	37	38	39	40
29	25	25	26	27	28	29	30	31	32	33	34	35	35	36	37	38
30	24	25	25	26	27	28	29	30	31	32	33	33	34	35	36	37
31	23	24	25	26	26	27	28	29	30	31	31	32	33	34	35	36
32	22	23	24	25	26	26	27	28	29	30	30	31	32	33	34	35

NUMBER OF TEETH ON REAR COG

Gear = (number of chainring teeth) × (tire diameter) ÷ (number of cog teeth).

This chart is based on a 700c wheel. Adapted from *Zinn and the Art of Road Bike Maintenance*, 4th ed. (VeloPress, 2013). Copyright © 2013 by Lennard Zinn.

	NUMBER OF TEETH ON FRONT CHAINRING												
43	44	45	46	47	48	49	50	51	52	53	54	55	56
103	106	108	110	113	115	118	120	122	125	127	129	132	134
95	97	99	101	103	106	108	110	112	114	117	119	121	123
87	89	91	93	95	97	99	101	103	106	108	110	112	114
81	83	85	87	89	90	92	94	96	98	100	102	23	106
76	77	79	81	83	84	86	88	90	91	93	95	97	98
71	73	74	76	77	79	81	82	84	86	87	89	91	92
67	68	70	71	73	74	76	78	79	81	82	84	85	87
63	64	66	67	69	70	72	73	75	76	78	79	81	82
60	61	62	64	65	67	68	69	71	32	74	75	76	78
57	58	59	61	62	63	65	66	67	69	70	71	73	74
54	55	57	58	59	60	62	63	64	65	67	68	69	70
52	53	54	55	56	58	59	60	61	62	64	65	66	67
49	50	52	53	54	55	56	57	58	60	61	62	63	64
47	48	49	51	52	53	54	55	56	57	58	59	60	62
45	46	47	49	50	51	52	53	54	55	56	57	58	59
44	45	46	47	48	49	50	51	52	53	41	55	56	57
42	43	44	45	46	47	48	49	50	51	43	53	54	55
41	41	42	43	44	45	46	47	48	49	50	51	52	53
39	40	41	42	43	0	45	45	46	47	48	49	50	51
38	39	40	40	41	42	43	44	45	46	47	47	48	49
37	37	38	39	40	41	42	43	43	44	45	46	47	48
35	36	37	38	39	40	40	41	42	43	44	45	45	46

INDEX

ABOUT THE AUTHORS

JAMIE SMITH spent four years as a military policeman in the U.S. Air Force stationed in Michigan's snowy Upper Peninsula. Though it may sound glamorous, it was actually a tedious duty making sure that no one snuck off with a B-52 Stratofortress tucked under his coat. To relieve the boredom, he began writing short stories to make his coworkers laugh. None of those early writing samples survive, however, as his coworkers would eventually burn the stories to keep themselves warm.

He spent several years as a municipal spin doctor for a sleepy Detroit suburb, receiving one Emmy nomination and several Telly Awards. Writing repetitive press releases and boring speeches inspired him to find something more exciting to write about: bike racing.

Today, Jamie is an active racer who gets nervous waiting at the start line of a bike race but feels fine after the first few pedal strokes. He is also a bike race announcer who enjoys translating the complexities of bike racing for befuddled spectators.

He has also taken on the role of coach to translate the complexities of bike racing for befuddled bike racers who mistakenly chase down their own teammates, miss the winning breakaway, and consistently finish one place out of the money.

His first book, *Roadie: The Misunderstood World of a Bike Racer*, was selected as a 2009 Notable Book by the Library of Michigan.

He currently lives in Rochester, Michigan, with his 11 bikes, 2 surfboards, 1 rowing scull, and 5 pair of cross-country skis.

BRAD KAMINSKI

CHRIS HORNER is one of cycling's most popular and observant riders, blessed with a rare ability to read a race in progress and describe it fluently afterward. He began his long pro career in the U.S. in 1995 with PAA-NutraFig; moved to Europe for three years with Française des Jeux; and then returned to America to guide the Mercury, Prime Alliance, Saturn, and Webcor teams, with whom he won nearly every major race on the domestic calendar.

A three-time national racing calendar champion, winner of the Tour de Langkawi, the Tour de Georgia, the Tour of the Basque Country, and the Tour of California, Horner led the 2012 U.S. Olympic squad and currently rides for RadioShack-Leopard-Trek, where his veteran counsel and unflappable temper make him the go-to guy for tactics, race smarts, and planning. You can follow Chris's career on his website, www.chrishornerracing.com, and Twitter (@hornerakg).

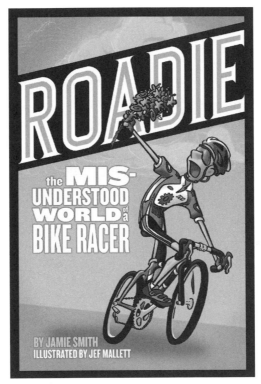